TOTAL RISK

Total Risk

*Nick Leeson and the Fall
of Barings Bank*

JUDITH H. RAWNSLEY

HarperBusiness
A Division of HarperCollins*Publishers*

This book was originally published in Great Britain in 1995 by HarperCollins Publishers under the title *Going for Broke*.

HarperCollins books may be purchased for educational, business, or sales promotional use. For information please write: Special Markets Department, HarperCollins Publishers, Inc., 10 East 53rd Street, New York, NY 10022.

FIRST U.S. EDITION

ISBN 0-88730-781-7

95 96 97 98 99 GB/HC 10 9 8 7 6 5 4 3 2 1

FOR JEREMY, WITH LOVE

Contents

Acknowledgements

I would like to thank those directors and employees of Barings, both past and present, who gave generous help in the writing of this book. Due to the sensitivity of the topic, many of those interviewed have requested anonymity; thank you all the same, your assistance was invaluable. I am particularly indebted to all those who were so willing to allow me to relate tales about their experiences at Barings, confirming that the tremendous of spirit of good humour that always prevailed in the firm lives on. My thanks go also to Toby Eady, Alexandra Pringle and Victoria Hobbs for getting the project off the ground and keeping it in the air, and to Michael Fishwick, Kirsten D. Sandberg, Anne O'Brien and HarperCollins for their guidance. A special mention goes to the staff of the Oriental Club for feeding and watering me, fielding phone calls, searching for lost notebooks and generally running around after me. Last but by no means least, a heartfelt thank you to my family for their unerring support and advice.

Illustrations

CARTOONS

Author's Foreword

'When you join Barings, you pick up the ball and run with it.' This piece of advice offered to me by one of the Tokyo analysts, as it was to many other new recruits during Baring Securities' formative years, could not have been more appropriate. Nothing could have prepared me for what I encountered when I began working for the company in Japan in March 1988. It was a firm of which one came to expect the unexpected.

The first clue might have been my interview at the firm's gleaming Portsoken Street headquarters in Bishopsgate, London. At the time, I was working as a journalist for a Japanese newspaper and, frankly, looking for a ticket to Japan. Having met a girl at a Christmas party who had just returned from a temporary posting in the Barings' Tokyo office, I had written to the Branch Manager there and been invited for an interview in London. After a wait of some forty minutes, a Japanese warrant trader entered the room and presented me with a wad of Japanese language material which she asked me to translate. I politely pointed out that it was clear on my curriculum vitae that, although I had a smattering of the language, I could not read or write it; that I was there to be interviewed for the position of editor of English language research. She seemed hugely embarrassed at this, and explained: 'Ah, you see, we couldn't lay our hands on your cv.' She then disappeared for another ten minutes, after which I was ushered in for a chat with Andrew Baylis, the Deputy Chairman of Baring Securities Limited. Though the conversation meandered rather, I must have displayed the requisite dose of 'hunger' – though at the time I had no idea what 'to be hungry' meant. I left feeling that the interview had been a shambles. Three weeks later I was on a plane heading for Japan.

* * *

In the second half of the Eighties Baring Securities, the entrepreneurial subsidiary of the conservative merchant bank, hired a large number of very young people, a fair proportion of whom had little financial experience, but who showed promise, drive and initiative. Those who learnt quickly were rewarded with vastly increased responsibility and swiftly rose to new heights; an opportunity for self-advancement which was among the best in the financial industry, even during a period of dramatic growth.

One of those late-Eighties recruits was myself and another was Nick Leeson. Our paths were to cross in Japan, when Leeson, stationed in Singapore, came to visit the Tokyo office. If someone had told me then that Nick was the man who would one day bring down Britain's oldest merchant bank, I would have laughed. It was as unbelievable as the idea that any of my friends and colleagues in the company would find themselves at the epicentre of such a notorious crisis.

I left Barings in 1992 to resume my journalistic career, by which time it had expanded far beyond the small company I had joined four years earlier and Nick Leeson was already making a name for himself in Singapore. However, I remained very close to many friends within Barings and the industry as a whole, both in Asia and London. Working for Barings had always been more like being part of a family than a company, which is why it came as such a personal blow when the bank collapsed. It triggered a series of conversations with friends around the world in which we discussed why it had happened, and it was with the support and encouragement of those friends that I set out to write this book.

I have endeavoured here to explain and describe the events and attitudes that formed the skeleton of the company, and the characters that gave it its flesh and made it grow. It is typical for people, especially in the financial industry, to be wise with the benefit of hindsight, but nevertheless, many of those I know who still work at Barings agree that, in the words of one London managing director, the events of February 1995 were 'an accident waiting to happen'.

TOTAL RISK

Introduction

At the time of its crash, Barings was regarded as one of the world's most pre-eminent financial institutions, the archetypal blue-blooded bank. Traditionally comparable with other family-controlled City institutions such as Rothschilds or Hambros, Barings had developed beyond its peers to successfully challenge the might of much larger banks like the British clearers Barclays and NatWest and the US institutions Morgan Stanley and Merrill Lynch, as an emerging markets specialist. The quality of its reputation was all the more remarkable for the fact that, by present day standards, it was a very modestly capitalized company; at year-end 1993 IBCA recorded Barings' total assets as £5.9 billion and its equity as £309.4 million, compared to Barclays Bank plc's £163 billion and £5.98 billion or NatWest's £152 billion and £5.89 billion. In its early days, Baring Brothers, the original merchant banking arm of the company, had blazed a trail into new financial markets and products which many, now more familiar, banking names were to follow only decades later. It was one of the few British banks that still maintained its independence and, over two hundred years after its foundation, the founders' direct descendants were still at the helm.

London's oldest established merchant bank had come very close to bankruptcy a hundred years before its ultimate demise. Financier to the British Empire and confidant of foreign governments, Barings faced near ruin in 1890 following heavy investment in the Americas. In the late Victorian age, South America held the same appeal for speculators as did the tiger economies of the Pacific Rim in the early 1990s. Barings had already lost money in Latin America on several occasions, but had also profited greatly and, never a firm to turn down a money-making opportunity, it was enticed to invest more. By 1890, under the guidance of Chairman Edward Revelstoke – a man who, blinded by profits, had thrown caution to the wind – Baring Brothers had raised £95 million for overseas borrowers with Argentina at the top of its list.

Chief amongst Barings' difficulties was the flotation of the Buenos Aires Water Supply and Drainage Company in 1888, a laudable company which aimed to make healthy profits from taking away sewage and supplying fresh water. By 1890, Revelstoke had committed Barings to a series of enormous payments on the project with no certainty as to where the money was coming from; in the end the company could not find the cash. The flotation had been only partly underwritten and Barings was hopelessly exposed. Attempts to borrow from other banks quickly stalled. The disaster was compounded when a political crisis broke out in Argentina followed by revolution; the Argentine loan began to look distinctly shaky, with South American borrowers defaulting to create the bust that follows boom. Bank rates went up from 3 to 5 per cent to protect British gold reserves. Lombard Street was alive with rumours that a major house was in trouble.

Barings was forced to declare that its liabilities amounted to £21 million, more than twice the reserves of the Bank of England, and found itself teetering on the brink of ruin. 'Verily, "A great Nemesis overtook Croesus,"' wrote Tom Baring at the time.

Friends and family rallied round, offering their private fortunes to help bail the bank out. Legend has it that on hearing the news, T. C. Baring (who had left the firm because he disapproved of Revelstoke's speculation in Argentina) went to the Bank of England, withdrew all his cash and securities, then hurried to Bishopsgate with several bulging Gladstone bags. The dramatic gesture was marred only by the fact that one of the bags burst open, the contents spilling out into the street, whilst Baring was arguing with the cab driver over an alleged charge of sixpence.

The family's fortunes were insufficient to save Barings, but there were others in 1890 who could not afford to let the bank fail. A century ago it was thought that the collapse of Barings would have set the City's dominoes tumbling and brought ruin to many more; '. . . at this moment the House of Baring is the keystone of English commercial credit and its collapse would provoke terrible consequences for English trade in all parts of the world,' wrote Baron Alphonse to Lord Rothschild. The City judged it the worst financial crisis there since the South Sea Bubble in 1720. Queen Victoria noted in her diary: 'Lord Revelstoke had rashly and credulously put all he had into these Argentine mines or works, and had been cheated by the Argentine agents who had come to him.'

In London, although the Barings was generally condemned for its speculation, the feeling was one of solidarity among financial institutions. The Bank of England organized a bail-out and Barings' rivals rallied to its rescue and, so they believed, to their own. Barings was saved, but at a catastrophic cost of £17.1 million (the equivalent of approximately £450 million today). The family was forced to retrench – selling off its silver and sacking its under-butlers – but they and their bank had survived. The only scar to be seen was the tell-tale comma in Baring Brothers and Co., Limited, the successor to the original partnership.

Within four years Barings had discharged its debt and, despite the catastrophe and ensuing humiliation, had resumed its position as one of the most powerful banking houses in Europe. Whereas in 1891 Alice James was advised by her house agent that the bank's name was unacceptable as a credit reference, by 1903 a German diplomat was able to report to Berlin: 'Anyone who wants to place a loan in London on a grand scale must apply to the Barings.'

Originally from the Netherlands, the Baring family moved to Bremen in North Germany from where Johann Baring emigrated to England in 1717. He married a local girl and settled down to conduct a modest business as a wool merchant. The venerable bank of yesterday found its roots in the cloth manufacturing and trading partnership set up by the family in 1762 and run by Johann's three sons: John, Charles and Francis.

It was Francis, the most entrepreneurial of the sons, who steered the family into merchant banking. Not content to stick to their

"SAME OLD GAME!"

OLD LADY OF THREADNEEDLE STREET. "YOU 'VE GOT YOURSELVES INTO A NICE MESS WITH YOUR PRECIOUS '*SPECULATION!*' WELL—I'LL HELP YOU OUT OF IT,—*FOR THIS ONCE!!!*"

homespun fare, in 1776 he broke away from the encumbrances of his brothers and set his sights firmly on finance, rapidly expanding from merely financing the wool trade into shipping and all aspects of international trade. Francis became a director and eventually chairman of the East India Company and having been elected to Parliament was created a baronet by William Pitt in 1793.

One of Francis's greatest achievements was bringing Barings into association with the Amsterdam house of Hope & Co., at that time one of the richest and most powerful in Europe and therefore in the world. The relationship was to last from 1766, when the two houses first corresponded, to far into the twentieth century, when Hopes became part of MeesPierson. Ironically, the present-day owner of MeesPierson is the Dutch banking conglomerate ABN Amro that was one of Barings' suitors after its crash.

Sir Francis set a precedent for future generations. His son Alexander travelled to the fledgling United States of America, married into its emergent high society, and capitalized on the business relationships established by his father and boosted by his new family connections. In 1803 Barings, in conjunction with Hopes, negotiated the repurchase of Louisiana by the Americans from Napoleon; in effect, Barings were the legal owners of Louisiana for a brief period when the state comprised the entire Mississippi valley. Alexander Baring came home to be created the first Lord Ashburton and appointed Chancellor of the Exchequer.

Through Barings' increasingly close relationship with Hopes, the house was able to expand its lending activities to foreign governments. In Europe, the Barings arranged loans to France for reparations after Waterloo. In the heyday of the British Empire, the Barings financed every major commodity from Malayan rubber to Australian wool, along with the ships that carried the produce of the colonies and dominions to Britain. Such was their influence in the high Victorian age that the Duc de Richelieu, French soldier and statesman, was moved to comment in 1818 that 'there are six great powers in Europe: England, France, Prussia, Austria, Russia and Baring Brothers.'

By utilizing his American family connections, Alexander brought Barings almost all the monetary agency, public and private, of the United States, together with a vast amount of mercantile business from individual Americans. Consequently for many years Barings 'held such balances of American money that they were enabled to exercise great influence not only in New York, but even over the monetary affairs of Europe,' *The Times* insisted in 1848. Within the decade, Barings also held accounts for Russia, Norway, Austria, Chile, Buenos Aires and New Granada, and the colonies of Canada,

Nova Scotia, New Brunswick and Australia. Personal accounts were held by Napoleon III of France and King Leopold of Belgium.

When the Depression hit Britain in the 1920s, forcing many companies out of business and many people out of a job, Baring Brothers was one of the few merchant banks that actively restructured and refinanced British companies. This activity marked the beginning of the bank's later and better-established move into corporate finance, a part of its banking business which focused on advising companies, agencies and sometimes governments about money matters, with specific reference to the acquisition or sale of assets in the form of companies. Barings attracted particular credit in the early Sixties for successfully advising Courtaulds in their fierce resistance to a takeover bid from ICI.

The worldwide demand for financing from governments and corporations developed so dramatically by way of the bond markets through the Fifties, Sixties and Seventies that this style of raising money led to the development of an entirely new specialization within the corporate finance field, now commonly referred to as capital markets. Barings was an active manager of new issues of equity and debt securities for UK issuers in the Sixties and Seventies and featured among those London houses that took part in the development of the Eurobond market. It led sterling debt issues for the World Bank, the InterAmerican Development Bank and the Government of Japan.

As the securities markets grew more complex and the amount of money available for investment increased, Barings set up an asset management arm, Baring Asset Management, which provided a range of fund and asset management services for pension funds, corporations and individuals.

One of the more unorthodox transformations in the life of Barings took place in 1969 when a majority stake in the equity of the business was transferred to the newly formed Baring Foundation and the bank changed from being a family-owned concern to one owned by a Charity. In 1985 a major recapitalization took place and the final 26 per cent stake in Barings was transferred, giving the East London charity complete ownership, but not control, of the new holding company called Barings plc. Control of the policy of the Barings Group, in the shape of one hundred voting shares, remained with the directors of Barings plc, while the economic interest in its equity was owned by the Foundation which applied the flow of dividends to charitable purposes. Although the move was done for financial reasons – as a means of avoiding existing inheritance tax laws and the possibility of a wealth tax being introduced by the ruling Labour Government – the Baring Foundation was a significant social benefactor, handing out £8.7 million in 1993 to a wide range of national and other charities with particular emphasis on social welfare. Many thought it ironical in the late Eighties that Baring Securities – Barings' most recent acquisition – could boast in one breath that it was one of the most successful securities companies, run by one of the highest paid executives in Britain, and was at the same time a generous charitable institution.

Barings had been through many metamorphoses in the course of its long history, surviving by adapting itself to changing circumstances, pushing headlong into new businesses and occasionally taking risks. The most significant change in the history of the bank took place in May 1984 when Baring Brothers paid just £6 million for a tiny stockbroking company called Henderson Crosthwaite (Far East), a niche player in the developing Far Eastern stock markets. It was to prove an inspired purchase, transforming the bank's fortunes during the Eighties, but in it lay a future that was to seal the fate of the house of Barings.

Two centuries ago, Francis Baring chose to ignore his mother's advice not to venture into the fledgling world of merchant banking. Warning of the perils ahead, in March 1766 she wrote:

> [I] advise you to be careful you do not run out of your depth. I am satisfied 'tis attended with risk and many houses called considerable abroad have often disappointed and sometimes absolutely ruined those who have placed Confidence in them . . . let Mr Touchet's [to whom Francis had been apprenticed]

example of grasping at too much and not being contented with a very handsome profit which he might have had without running such enormous risks, be a warning to you.

Francis Baring was to prove his mother's fears unfounded. His descendants were not to be so lucky.

1 | King of SIMEX

Nick Leeson woke in his spacious fifth-floor apartment. It was 6.15 a.m. on Thursday, 23 February 1995. He went through his morning ritual of shower and shave mechanically, kissed Lisa good-bye and then took the elevator down.

Outside the heat was already searing, wrapping around him like a hot, moist towel as he walked towards Orchard Boulevard. The neatly manicured lawns and flower beds which bordered the quiet road were bright in the sunshine. Tamil and Malay workers, their heads shaded by hats, had begun to clip hedges and wash cars.

On Orchard Boulevard, a wide, tree-lined avenue, Nick hailed one of Singapore's smart sky blue government-owned COMFORT cabs. Slumped in the back, he stared nonchalantly at the slogan displayed on the dashboard: *Caring, Observant, Mindful, Friendly, Obliging, Responsible, Tactful – I am the best person for this job and no one else can provide this service better*, a description which many in Barings would have applied to Nick himself.

His life revolved around just one small area of Singapore, in itself a tiny, tropical island. The drive from his home in the exclusive Angullia Park, past the ritzy shopping malls of Orchard Road, past palm-filled gardens and refurbished colonial buildings, to the business district, took only ten minutes, even though the traffic was already building. The cab pulled up outside Raffles Place at the heart of the business district, a neat pedestrian area with modern sculptures and raised grass areas surrounded by glass and chrome skyscrapers. Businessmen and office workers were already thronging out of the MRT and grabbing coffees and pastries on the way to their offices.

Alighting from the cab, he strode quickly across the corner of Raffles Place in the sunshine. Milling among the businessmen, Nick was distinguishable only because he was Western. Of medium height and stocky build with thinning, light brown hair, in his white shirt and suit trousers he looked like any other twenty-eight-year-old British stockbroker. The only distinctive feature was the striped jacket he carried in his hand.

He pushed on the heavy glass door of the Overseas Union Bank centre and crossed the lobby. A short ride in the elevator took him up to the SIMEX trading floor to prepare for the battle ahead. It was 7.30 a.m., but inside the exchange it could have been any time of day or night; as in a casino, the lighting was artificial and air conditioning kept the temperature at a constant neutral. It was a relief to be in the cool.

The football-pitch sized floor was already hectic as some four hundred traders, mostly Asian men, scurried around exchanging market news in readiness for the onslaught. Phones were ringing and floor assistants were busy preparing sheets of trading positions and order cards. Most of the traders were hanging around their booths on the periphery of the trading floor, chatting on the telephone, their umbilical cord to colleagues in the office and clients. The booths were a clutter of paperwork, ticket machines and computer screens on top of which sat mascots and numerous bottles of water.

Nick walked swiftly across the floor to his own booth which sported a wilting Union Jack. Even in their rush his colleagues and fellow SIMEX traders took time to greet him. He was, after all, one of the most pivotal figures on the exchange. Out on the street, Nick was just another ex-pat businessman, but on the SIMEX floor he was King. Barings accounted for a high proportion of the market's turnover and Nick had an overriding influence on the market. Rival traders constantly monitored his positions to see how the market might move against them.

He spent a few minutes skimming through the news monitors and checking the trading position sheets, then clicked on the squawk box, a permanently open lease line: 'How's life?'

'You're in especially good spirits today aren't you?' replied

Fernando Gueler, Head Proprietary Derivatives Trader in Tokyo. Fernando, a young Californian who talked faster than anyone could listen, had been speaking to Nick over the squawk box like this for years. On visits to Tokyo Nick had always got on well with his trading counterparts and had proved a welcoming host when they visited him in Singapore. The team had been working together at Barings for five years and the feeling of solidarity between them had increased over the last twelve months as they had become compatriots in the firm's most profitable venture.

After the usual market rundown, they went through some positions then spent a few minutes chatting about where they had both been out the night before. As usual Leeson had been down to Harry's, his favourite bar just a short walk away from SIMEX on Boat Quay, where he had enjoyed a few beers with his fellow ex-pat traders and listened to the usual jazz combo pumping out a blend of soulful and hip-hop tunes. Adrian, another of Nick's trading counterparts in Tokyo, interrupted Fernando for a quick chat – the usual banter about the respective merits of Bolton Wanderers and Watford – then Nick clicked off.

As the crescendo on the trading floor mounted, Nick slipped on his trading jacket and, armed with a handful of order cards and a pencil, waded into the Nikkei 225 pit ready for the 8 a.m. opening bell.

As the market came alive, the pit became a rugby scrum of traders furiously signalling and shouting. The noise was deafening. The trading floor was a kaleidoscope of colour, the local traders in their traditionally auspicious red jackets contrasting vividly against the bolder, zanier colours favoured by the overseas traders: Barclays Bank in red-and-white stripes with blue eagles on the back, Standard Chartered in purple and yellow, Morgan Stanley in pale green, Yamaichi purple with apple green trim, and Nomura a more sober grey. While the traders punched the air and yelled orders at each other across the pit, runners in vivid yellow ran between the pit and the booths with order cards. SIMEX officials in sky blue officiated the whole process, which was much more orderly than it looked, while microphones and close circuit TVs dangling from the ceiling recorded every trade. Above their heads, digital screens and TV monitors flashed out real time prices and the latest world news which might affect the markets.

On the surface everything appeared normal that Thursday morning in February. Nick seemed as sharp as usual. Standing on the steps of the hexagonal yellow pit executing the orders hand-signalled to him by his floor staff in the Barings booth, he cut a striking figure in his navy-and-gold trading jacket. Although many of the Asian traders were big, Nick was not only taller, but louder and more aggressive than most of them, his voice carrying further than even the shrill tones of the few Asian women on the floor. It was his unwavering self-certainty which had made him into a trader who was both revered and feared in the pit.

From time to time Nick dashed back to the Barings booth and chatted with his team members and clients. He seemed cheerful to everyone that morning, despite complaining of a stomach upset which forced him to run out to the toilets whenever the market went slack. It had become a standing joke that he always seemed to have one. His Asian colleagues all presumed that he must be looking forward to his birthday celebrations. Nick was the picture of calm, the relaxed guy they all knew.

Internally, however, the tension was mounting, a taut wire which threatened to snap. Glancing up at the prices flashing on the Nikkei screen overhead, Nick dashed off the floor. Taking a couple of minutes out in the toilets, he tried to cope with his emotions and wondered silently how the day would end. Only a month earlier it had seemed as if nothing could go wrong for him; he was the firm's star trader, admired by colleagues and managers alike for the profits he was reaping for the benefit of all in the firm. His judgment of the market had seemed infallible. Then on 17 January the great Hanshin earthquake had struck Japan and the Nikkei stock index had started plunging.

Although Nick, like many in Barings, was a self-made man who had risen up through the ranks to assume a position of great responsibility, he had one secret which he had been keeping discreetly hidden. For several months he had been taking increasing bets on the Nikkei's direction which, during the last few weeks, had ballooned to epic proportions. Throughout February those covert positions had been haemorrhaging millions in losses. For once everyone in the market had been right, except him. Swilling his mouth out with cold water, he gathered his thoughts together and returned to the pit, trading as normal despite the fact that the Nikkei index continued to plummet.

Later that morning Tony Railton, Senior Settlements Clerk from Barings London, tracked Nick down on the floor to ask him about an unexplained $190 million hole in his trading account which they had touched upon briefly the night before. Railton – seconded to Singapore to cover a colleague's maternity leave – had identified some big problems but Nick was proving difficult to pin down. That morning was no different; not only was the floor crowded and noisy but Nick insisted on continuing to trade as they talked. There was no hope of a serious discussion. Railton gave up.

After the final bell at 2.15 p.m., Nick returned to his booth and called his wife, telling her he desperately needed to talk things over, that he could no longer cope. She suggested that they go away on their own for a few days. He then made a quick call to one of his friends, apologizing for the fact that he wouldn't be able to make the trip to Phuket; Lisa had decided to take him for a quiet weekend away to celebrate his birthday instead. Putting down the phone, he gathered up his trading cards and papers and calmly walked off the SIMEX floor. Nick Leeson had made his final trade.

While his wife wondered why he sounded so distraught, Nick spent the next hour buying his colleagues drinks in a bar called Escape. They played pinball, joked about a *Mr Bean* video and snacked on junk food. To his colleagues, Nick seemed his usual cool self. After lunch, Nick sat down with Railton at last. Simon Jones, the aggressively territorial Operations Manager for South Asia, joined them. They discussed the missing dollars for some twenty minutes, then Nick left the room. He never came back.

Nick's disappearance from the Barings' offices in Ocean Towers caused a commotion that afternoon. It wasn't just Railton who needed to speak to him. Coopers & Lybrand, Barings' auditors, were hoping to meet with him to clear up some outstanding questions before they signed off on their audit. The grandfatherly Tony Hawes was also trying to get hold of Nick from Tokyo. Hawes, Barings Group Treasurer, who had been unable to see Leeson when he was in Singapore a few weeks earlier, was now about to return from his side trip. He needed to speak to Nick about funding problems. Office staff began to ring around.

As night fell and there was still no sign of Nick, word was passed to London that there was a big reconciliation problem but the trader couldn't be found. In the early hours of Friday morning, Hawes – who had just landed in Singapore – and Railton went back to the offices to start looking at the accounts themselves. They were joined there shortly afterwards by Jones and Bax, the Regional Operations Manager for South Asia, who had been dragged out of bed. Hawes started to examine a computer print-out and noticed a previously unknown account numbered 88888 with thousands of transactions on it, all seemingly running enormous losses.

As the one man who could answer their questions still couldn't be found, the team frantically sifted through Nick's trading positions and searched filing cabinets to find the answers for themselves. But as the night wore on the questions simply multiplied.

At two the following morning in Tokyo, Fernando Gueler was woken by a call from London. Fernando, a hyperactive thirty-year-old, had been out for a few drinks the night before celebrating the fact that, as head of one of Baring's most profitable operations, he had just been told he was to be made a director of the firm. It was Mary Walz on the line. Fernando was used to the occasional midnight call from London but, even though the American woman was always intense, there was an edge to her voice that alarmed him. 'There's something wrong in Singapore. Something funny's going on with the margin money. I can't get in touch with Nick. Can you try his portable?'

Fernando got on the phone immediately, but there was no reply from either Nick's portable or his home. He tried consistently for the next hour, then gave up and went back to his futon, presuming that Nick was still out drinking and that it was a problem which could wait until the morning. He slept fitfully, however, as thoughts of unknown problems tossed like flotsam through his mind.

At 6.30 a.m. the phone rang again. It was Mary: 'Get to the ⌐fice as quick as you can. Prepare all the customer positions in Singapore and report back to me on Norris's line.'

Panic set in as Fernando imagined that Nick had unexpectedly quit to join Merrill Lynch or Morgan Stanley, Barings' rivals on SIMEX. In the absence of any other problem that sprang to mind and in the light of his new appointment, it even crossed his mind that it might all be a practical joke, a kind of directorial initiation ceremony.

When he got to the office he called Mary back. It was still only seven and the office was quiet with just a few of the Japanese office girls preparing pots of coffee and faxing out the morning news. Peter Norris, Barings' Chief Executive Officer, picked up the phone. He had been in the office for over sixteen hours but was as incisive as usual. 'Go into the conference room on your own. I'll call you there. We need to talk to you.'

The phone rang on the grey boardroom table as Fernando entered the room. 'Sit down Fernando and listen to what I have to say. Don't interrupt me until I've finished. We have reason to believe that Nick Leeson has left Singapore and that he's left us with outstanding positions of large size. The guys in Singapore have been working all night long. They've been collecting all the positions, which they'll fax through to you. We need you to measure the delta sensitivity of these positions. When you've done it, call me. And don't tell anyone.'

As Fernando left the conference room he passed the Branch Manager's office and poked his head round the door. William Daniel was at his desk sipping his first coffee and shuffling through papers. 'Have you heard that something's wrong in Singapore?' Daniel nodded, but it was clear from the relative calm on his face that he didn't know how serious the situation was.

The print-outs of all Barings' positions were already spewing out of the fax machine when Fernando got back to his desk. Glancing through them he knew immediately that something was wrong. The sheets were covered with positions that didn't belong to

Barings. They belonged to Nick's biggest client, a client which had been putting orders through Barings in such large size that he had requested anonymity, not only in the rest of the market, but also among all Baring staff except the trader he dealt with directly – Nick. Fernando had spent much of the previous week fending off financial journalists pestering him as to who this client might be.

He punched the positions into a spread sheet on his computer and used his calculator to work out the net sensitivity, but the result was already obvious. For the last few weeks he, along with every other trader in the market, had been calculating daily how much the holder of these particular positions had been losing on a mark-to-market basis. He had already made his own guesstimate of a loss of $250 million.

As the computer screen blinked ever-increasing negative numbers, another working day dawned in the office around him. Benjamin and Adrian, Fernando's fellow traders, came in with coffee and newspapers; one of the secretaries was talking about a new restaurant she had tried the night before. Over the last few months a great feeling of camaraderie had grown among the members of the Tokyo arbitrage team. Everyone on the desk was in good spirits that morning. Not only was it Friday, but the team were, like all Barings' employees worldwide, expecting to be told that weekend the bonuses they had been awarded for their last year's work. Fernando's team hoped to be well rewarded for the hefty contribution they had made to the firm's bottom line.

At around 8.30 a.m. the Singapore office called to check that Fernando had received their faxes. He quizzed them about the odd positions and was told that Singapore had already been in touch with the head of SIMEX; Barings' net positions at the exchange apparently added up to what the company believed it had, *plus* the positions which everyone thought belonged to the client.

'What *is* this?' Fernando questioned. 'These belong to Nick's client. We weren't clearing for him.'

'We don't know who they belong to.'

A sudden fear overwhelmed him, but the normality of everyone's behaviour around him when there was a problem on such a colossal scale made it all seem surreal. Still certain that there must be some mistake, he had begun to double-check the numbers when Norris called back and told him that they had uncovered some more futures positions. 'Fernando, forget everything else for the moment and look at the futures. Ignoring the futures positions on SIMEX, if we only had the long Osaka position, what would the P&L be on that leg alone?'

'Down $450 million.' There was a deadly silence. 'Peter, these positions belong to Nick's client.'

'Fernando, there *is* no client.'

2 | Fall Out

'Yes, I'm the man you want.'
NICK LEESON

By Friday the alarm bells were ringing loud and clear in London. For Barings' Chairman, the call came at 7.15 that morning. It was Peter Norris on the line. Peter Baring was awoken from what must have been a blissful sleep; only the Wednesday before, the Barings board had met to peruse the draft accounts which showed a small rise in profits – a healthy result in what, for most, had been a sickly year. One of the biggest contributors to those profits had been the supposedly lucrative derivatives trading operation in Tokyo that was supported by the futures operation in Singapore.

Norris had spent the last 24 hours finding out how bad the situation was. Early on Thursday, Norris had received a call from Tony Gamby, Settlements Director in London, in turn alerted by Railton in Singapore, informing him that the firm's star trader had disappeared, leaving behind him a huge financial time bomb. A bomb big enough to blow Barings to bits.

Within the hour, the Chairman and Norris had gathered the bank's top brass at eight Bishopsgate at the heart of the city. The firm's three chief executives had much to lose. Baring was due to retire within months after a long and distinguished career at the bank; Andrew Tuckey, Barings' Deputy Chairman, was expecting to steer the company into its future as an integrated investment bank and Norris, his right-hand man, was hoping to step up into his shoes.

Although the details of the problem were still sketchy, the outline was clear; the company was in deep trouble. In the face of such a financial storm, a City institution has only one port of call: the Bank of England. So, as his forefathers had done in 1890 when

Barings teetered on the brink of bankruptcy after betting too heavily in Argentina, Peter Baring made a grim call to the Old Lady of Threadneedle Street to say he had an urgent problem.

Eddie George, the Governor of the Bank of England, had just departed for a skiing holiday in the French resort of Avoriaz in Haute-Savoie. In his absence, his deputy, Rupert Pennant-Rea, the former *Economist* editor, stepped in to take charge of affairs along with Brian Quinn, Executive Director in charge of banking super-vision. It was to be Pennant-Rea's first and last opportunity to do so. Only weeks after Barings' collapse, Pennant-Rea's own career was derailed by revelations of an affair with a former colleague from the *Economist* which had reputedly taken place within the Bank's hallowed halls.

Peter Baring walked the short distance to the Bank of England a shaken man. A highly regarded financier in the City, who only hours earlier had upheld an untarnished reputation for reliability and caution, he now had to explain to the Bank that it faced its worst crisis in history. Baring explained the problem to Pennant-Rea and Quinn in typically understated tones, giving his first estimate of the losses – at this stage a little over £400 million. The positions that Leeson had built up were still open and so Barings still carried the risk of further market declines; the futures contracts for which Leeson had had such a penchant still had weeks to run, some of the options several months. The meeting was over in half an hour.

The phone calls to the wider world began shortly after. First to be called was Carol Sargeant (in charge of supervising UK banks), who immediately began to pull together a team to analyse Barings' potential losses. Next on the list was Eddie George who entered his chalet to hear the phone ringing. Before he had even had time to test the *piste*, he found himself taking a taxi back to Geneva and talking his way on to the next flight back to London.

The chairmen and chief executives of the major British merchant and clearing banks, many of whom were Barings' rivals, were then summoned to a meeting that afternoon without being told its pur-pose. Just as in 1890, the heads of the City's venerable old insti-tutions congregated in Threadneedle Street with their modern day cousins: Sir Chips Keswick of Hambros, Lord Rockley of Kleinwort

Benson, Sir David Scholey of S. G. Warburg, John Craven of Morgan Grenfell and a dozen other leading lights in the banking world. The first meeting was to consider the question of whether this problem was one which Barings had to shoulder alone or whether it could have a domino effect that would cause a crisis of confidence in other British banks and possibly even other foreign players in the City.

At 5 p.m. the same afternoon the bankers assembled in the Octagon room on the first floor of the Bank, a regal, high-ceilinged, eighteenth-century room. Taking their places around blue baize tables which had been arranged in a hollow square, beneath a sparkling chandelier, there was fierce speculation as to exactly who it was that was in trouble.

Pennant-Rea, Brian Quinn, Michael Foot [Quinn's deputy] and Carol Sargeant then trooped in. Pennant-Rea chaired the meeting and came swiftly to the point: cash. It wasn't simply a problem of short-term liquidity, but of solvency: Barings was on the point of going bust. The company needed to be recapitalized, but the big questions were: What was the cost and who was going to pay?

The meeting broke up before 6 p.m. and all present were requested to be on call throughout the weekend. That evening Kenneth Clarke, Chancellor of the Exchequer, was briefed about Barings' plight at Dorneywood, his country seat. The scale of the losses still could not be quantified as the positions remained open and further losses incurred if the market continued to decline when it re-opened on Monday morning. Both the Bank and Clarke agreed that bailing out this blue-blooded concern, however venerable, was not a justifiable use of public money so long as it was established that there was no general risk to the industry as a whole. Besides the practical issues, it would be difficult for Clarke to justify politically at a time of intense public opposition to the remuneration packages of senior management of privatized industries. But if the Bank wasn't prepared to write the 'blank cheque', it was going to be equally difficult for a private sector bank to justify the risk to its shareholders. The odds of Barings' survival were not looking favourable.

*   *   *

The Leeson's had left their fifth-floor apartment in Angullia Park the previous day. Their maid watched them leave carrying two suitcases. The couple were driven the twenty miles across town to Changi airport by Nick's best friend, a British trader on SIMEX, who was later to have his passport impounded for providing this chauffeur service. At 11.55 p.m. on Thursday night the Leesons checked into the Regent Hotel in Kuala Lumpur, the four-star hotel fraternized by Barings' executives when travelling to Malaysia. In a supreme stroke of black humour, Leeson demanded the company's negotiated discount room rate. Having filled in a registration card, omitting details of his onward travel, he was taken to a room on the VIP floor.

Just before noon on the Friday when Peter Baring was meeting with Pennant-Rea and Quinn, Leeson paid his bill by American Express. He and Lisa made the 45-minute taxi ride to Subang international airport where they hopped on a flight to Kota Kinabalu. They were met at the airport in Kota Kinabalu by a hotel car which took them to the Shangri-la's Tanjung Aru resort hotel located on the North coast of Borneo, bordering a tropical rain forest to the South.

The Shangri-la Tanjung Aru resort is the epitome of a luxury hotel. It has 500 rooms, most with majestic views across the South China Sea, vast marble floors and hand-carved wooden doors. It has discreet service, but above all, it is remote; the perfect hideaway for someone who wants to escape from the world. They checked in and a bell boy showed them to room 428, a RM$400-a-night (£120) Thai-style suite in the bougainvillaea-covered old wing, which has sweeping views from the balcony out across immaculate lawns fringed with pink and yellow frangipani trees, to the South China Sea. To hotel staff they appeared like any normal couple, looking forward to a peaceful holiday.

Throughout Saturday at Barings, the atmosphere was frenetic. The firm had called in Schroder Wagg, its financial advisers, and the firm's two top bankers George Mallinkrodt and Win Bischoff were working with senior staff to put together a recapitalization plan, a financial lifeboat to keep Barings afloat. Barings and the Bank of England had quickly and discretely alerted all those they considered might be potential buyers; the major banks of Europe, the US and other substantial institutional players were approached to see if they were interested in all or parts of the Barings Group and a stream of calls came back from interested parties. The bank's reputation, the quality of its staff and the goodwill of the business, despite the catastrophe, made Barings an attractive proposition. The UK corporate finance division, Baring Asset Management and the Asian research and equity broking operations, in particular, were highly sought after. The big problem remained the uncapped exposure to further losses, which seemed to make the organization of a collective lifeboat that would provide temporary liquidity more feasible in the short term.

That same day Bank of England envoys, who had been sent off around the world, worked with frantic Barings staff searching through Leeson's positions to establish the precise exposure to which Leeson had committed Barings. As more details came to light, so the known losses grew. By Saturday evening they were known to have reached some £625 million on a mark-to-market basis.

In an attempt to cap the losses, Barings and the Bank focused on the counterparties to Leeson's outstanding trades, in the hope that they could persuade a number of them to close out their positions at a price. This would at least reduce Barings' outstanding market liability and help to quantify and cap the overall losses. One American investment bank merely hung up the phone when asked. In the event it transpired that there were just too many small counterparties and insufficient time to contact them, so the positions and risk remained Barings'.

The next solution that was sought was to find an outsider, or group of outsiders, that would quote a price for taking on Barings' derivatives risk or had a vested interest in doing so. It was believed that the Japanese banks fell into the latter category, as they had an interest in stymieing a collapse of the Japanese stock market. The Bank of England approached the Bank of Japan directly, however, the ultimate decisions in Japan are made by the Japanese Ministry of Finance. MoF did not want to be seen helping out a foreign institution which had burnt its fingers by meddling around with the very derivatives it had tried to stifle and politely made it clear that local law prevented off-exchange dealings in derivatives. In other words, it serves you right. Another avenue had been closed.

By Sunday morning, first reports of the crisis, with estimates of the size of the losses, had already been transmitted on the BBC World service and had appeared in the Sunday papers. Fleet Street had got hold of the story the afternoon before, after what can only be construed as a rather bizarre tip-off by a senior Barings executive.

At 10 a.m. the bankers were due to reconvene at Threadneedle Street. In the ludicrous belief that secrecy needed to be maintained, they had been instructed to enter the bank via an entrance at the back, rather than through its imposing portals. Attempting to gain entrance, they banged on the door for several minutes, before trooping somewhat sheepishly round to the front in full view of a number 23 bus and a Double Decker whose upper deck carried an entourage of camera-clicking Japanese tourists, blissfully ignorant of the historical moment they were capturing on film, an event in which their own nation had unwittingly played such a vital part.

Back in the Octagon room, Eddie George was waiting. The Governor outlined the seriousness of the situation to the casually clothed bankers and their legal advisers. The City normally rallies round to protect its own and the bankers seemed willing to fork out to save the venerable Barings, but George made it clear that the chances of a rescue hung on a successful cap to the derivatives exposure. The only means of saving the bank was for all the banks present to contribute money to help float a lifeboat which would pour capital into Barings' punctured balance sheet and help it to sail on through the impending financial storm. There was an embarrassed shuffling and muttering about bottomless liabilities, a 'running for the hills' as one banker put it. Overnight, news agencies had asked market experts how the news would affect world markets in the morning and by Sunday everyone knew that the Nikkei 225 index would plummet because of the situation.

The whole world had already been told that Barings' current losses were £600 million and from the size of the positions quoted in the press it was easy to work out that for every percentage point fall in the Nikkei the loss was going to accumulate a further $70 million. Furthermore it was expected that without substantial assistance from the Japanese and Singaporean authorities the market was likely to open down 4 per cent or 5 per cent.

Eddie George told them that he understood their sentiment in not wanting to provide a cap for the derivatives exposure and proposed the creation of a three month lifeboat – effectively a bridging loan – with a sale to follow shortly after. Peter Baring, visibly distressed, then stood up and thanked the bankers for coming. He stressed his ignorance of the fact that there had been any trading irregularity until Friday 24 February and suggested that the problem had arisen as a result of dealings by a 'rogue trader'.

A presentation was then given on the various businesses of the Barings Group by Peter Norris, Andrew Tuckey and John Bolsover, Chairman and Chief Executive of Baring Asset Management. Unfortunately, John Bolsover, whose own business had not been responsible for the bank's demise, began his presentation with a five-minute speech about the need for the year's staff bonuses – a total payment of around £100 million – to be paid in order to avert a mass defection. Although this was a perfectly understandable request, given that he wanted to hold the bank together, the message stunned many in the audience and the mood shifted quite dramatically. When the team left, strong views were aired about what had been said on the bonus front. Many have since expressed the view that, particularly in light of management's own culpability for the bank's collapse, this was sheer arrogance. The group broke up for lunch.

When the banking consortium reconvened in the afternoon, Andrew Buxton, Chairman of Barclays Bank, assumed the role of arm twister as George and Pennant-Rea had departed to meet

Clarke at No.11 Downing Street. Buxton by all accounts did a good job, persuading even the more reluctant banks to throw some money into the pot in the cause of what he described as 'the future of the banking industry'. Although there was a rather inelegant discussion about what the individual banks would be getting in return for their help, by 2.30 p.m. when the Governor returned, everyone had contributed to make up a kitty of £600 million. At 3 p.m. the meeting was again adjourned.

Despite the £600 million raised, a cap still had to be found for the liabilities and the bankers needed a solution by 8pm London time when the Australian markets would open, followed by Tokyo a few hours later. There were few alternatives left, the most promising of which was the interest shown by the Sultan of Brunei, who held a large Japanese investment book and had been suggested as a possible saviour by John Bolsover. Early indications showed that he might be willing to take on the full risk of Barings' open positions and recapitalize the bank allowing it to continue business on Monday morning under new Asian ownership.

When the meeting resumed again at 7 p.m. it seemed as if there was a deal on the table that would work; one of the bankers commented that it seemed as if Father Christmas had come. Eddie George left the room to organize the final details.

At precisely 8.36 p.m. in London on Sunday 26 February 1995, Eddie George walked back into the room. 'I am very sorry gentlemen, our investor is not willing to proceed,' he apologized. He told the assembled group that they had come very close to a settlement, but that there just hadn't been sufficient time to impart the full details and achieve a sufficient level of understanding for the Sultan to be completely comfortable. Barings had gone into administration, the UK equivalent of the US's Chapter Eleven which would at least give them time to look for a solution to the losses before filing for bankruptcy. One of the Baring family stood up, but was so choked that he couldn't speak. Eddie George went off again to meet Kenneth Clarke at Downing Street, leaving the exhausted team to snack on wilting sandwiches and pizza ordered by the doorman. The casually attired bankers later slipped unnoticed through the awaiting hoard of paparazzi, who pounced upon the suited legal and financial advisers who followed them out.

Throughout the course of the weekend, despite the secrecy with which it was shrouded internally (and having overcome the notion that it was all a practical joke because their bonuses were due to be paid on Monday), a small proportion of Barings staff globally had begun to unravel the details of the bank's plight for themselves. Uncertain as to whether Barings would live to see another tomorrow, even under a different name, the victims of the management's failure, took consolation in the bottle at expensive bars and restaurants across the globe. From Harry's Bar in Singapore to the Captains Bar in the Mandarin Hotel in Hong Kong, to the new Philippe Starck restaurant across the water in Kowloon, to the New Otani Hotel in Tokyo and The Anchor Pub in London, cellars saw a sudden run on Dom Perignon and the cash registers rang to the tune of corporate credit cards. If the staff couldn't get their bonuses in monetary terms, they thought they'd better drink it, though the joke turned sour on Monday when it was discovered that the corporate credit cards had been cancelled.

By Sunday night, many of the firm's employees around the world had gone into their offices to check for news on the Reuter or Bloomberg screens. Those in parts of the world where news was more difficult to obtain, had read the papers faxed to them by friends and colleagues in London. The full measure of the situation was too shocking to comprehend; it would take days, if not weeks, for anxiety to set in. Right now, people were just in a state of stunned disbelief. In Tokyo the traders had spent the weekend pouring over sheets of positions they had never seen before and sleeping on the dealing room floor.

While most of the firm's employees held up remarkably well under the circumstances, panic was such in London, that events took a turn for the worse that Sunday evening. At Baring Securities London headquarters many long-standing employees had gathered to await the outcome of the bankers' meeting in the firm's dealing room. The call came at 9.15 p.m. The nearest employee picked up the phone to be told that the rescue attempt had fallen through. He stood up on one of the dealing desks and shouted only half-jokingly to the expectant crowd: 'The administrators are coming in. Grab what you can and run.'

Chaos ensued as some employees, over-reacting in the heat of the moment and imagining that the liquidators would be arriving any minute, began pulling things from shelves. People began to back up research data on computer disks and snatch client lists from drawers. Half a dozen husbands and wives, girlfriends and boyfriends drew up outside the Baring Securities offices at No. 1 America Square and helped their partners to load boxes into the backs of their cars. One girl was on her second trip when the receptionist stopped her: 'I've had a call. I'm not going to stop you this time, but no more.'

The same girl was on her third trip, loaded down with research files, when she came face to face with a group of senior executives headed by Henry Anstey in front of the revolving doors.

'This isn't yours. This is the property of Baring Securities research department. Put it back,' Anstey commanded. 'This is theft.'

'It's my work. You take it back,' she replied, throwing the whole lot on to the floor of the lobby, before she nipped out through the revolving doors to escape with the two loads she'd already secured.

The vast majority of Barings' employees turned up for work on Monday not knowing whether they had a job any longer. Many had spent the night in the office awaiting news. For once, this normally chatty, effervescent bunch were lost for words. As people arrived to be met with the news that the lifeboat had failed and that a death sentence had been passed on Barings, offices globally took on the aspect of morgues. Since Barings had stopped trading, there was nothing for anyone to do except sit around waiting for news and talking about what might or might not have happened. It is difficult to imagine how painful it must have been to be sitting in a silent office waiting for a Reuters screen to give you news of your own destiny. The adrenalin only started to surge again when Reuters posted an interview with Leeson's sister in which in which she said: 'He wasn't one of those public school types who had it all handed to him on a plate.' A rally went up from trading desks worldwide in response: 'No, the bastard took it for himself.' The fight back had begun.

The global round of Last Suppers which were accompanied by such mementos as specially made boxes of matches embossed with the epithet NICK LEESON'S BIG NIGHT OUT, spawned the beginning of a week of black humour, the kinds of jokes and comments that epitomize the English reaction to a seemingly hopeless situation. In London, staff began to organize Nick Leeson's farewell party and order sets of T-shirts with Nick Leeson's head on the front and alternately: 'Natural Born Killer' or 'I Fucked the Queen' on the back. A member of the Financial Products Group was captured on film wearing a T-shirt sporting the maxim FREE NICK LEESON . . . IT WOZ ONLY A BILLION SHAG! at the Hong Kong Rugby Sevens a month after the bank's crash. He was asked to report to the Barings box over the public announcement system. The first Nick Leeson jokes, however paltry, began to be bantered around offices globally, including the revamped Q: 'What's the difference between Elvis and Nick Leeson?' A: 'Nick Leeson's definitely dead' and the slightly more novel Q: 'What's the difference between O. J. Simpson and Nick Leeson?' A: 'O. J. Simpson knew when to cut his losses.' Despite their apparently negative tone, this attitude contributed greatly to lifting spirits and raising morale during a very difficult and uncertain time for everyone concerned.

By Tuesday morning the troops were showing a much greater degree of resilience and were uniting in the face of adversity. The real value in the company was in its staff and the more of them that stayed together, the better for everyone. Although in administration, it was hoped that a buyer could still be found for the whole company, and if not, that it would at least be sold off in a series of large parts. The management entrusted the staff not to jump ship, but to remain together at least until the end of the week, to give them a chance to seek an appropriate new owner. The employees gladly gave their commitment and this new resolve was captured in one of the equity salesman's morning meeting note of that day.

Nicholas William Leeson

Objective

To apply my proven ability to alter my employer's balance sheet, move international markets, and sway foreign exchange rates towards a trading position at a currently sound financial institution.

Experience

Barings plc (Singapore)

2/1/95–2/25/95

ROGUE DERIVATIVES TRADER

Instigated, oversaw, and operated an unauthorized futures trading strategy based on the Japanese Index. Specialized in open-ended, naked positions.

- Lost over $1.2 billion in one month in derivatives trading.
- Single-handedly destroyed a 233-year-old bank.
- Personally depressed the Nikkei average by 4%, and the Dow by 28 points.
- Solely devalued the British Pound against the US Dollar.

1993–1995

Leeson Securities – Las Vegas

MANAGING PARTNER

Founded and ran a renegade securities firm. Excelled in choosing stocks with minimum research. Primarily preyed on senior citizens and widows as clients.

- Churned retail accounts to generate over $800,000 per year in commissions.
- Created the Vegas Fund, a revolutionary concept in money management. Invested fund assets by taking positions in randomly occurring statistical events at Caesar's Palace.
- Ran a satelite operation targeted at sports fans interested in investing in teams of their choice.

Education
1989–1993

International Correspondence Schools
Cum Lousey, Sextuple-majored in Business Administration, Book-keeping, Accounting, Learning the personal Computer, Veterinary Assistant, and TV/VCR Repair.

- Teaching Assistant to Betty Boop
- Only person to actually call their 800 number.

Interests

Short sales, naked puts, bungee jumping, travelling incognito through Malaysia.

References

Gordon 'greed is good' Gekko

One Barings employee, realizing that Leeson would soon be in need of a new job, kindly drew up a new and entirely fanciful curriculum vitae on his behalf.

Tuesday 28th
CAPTAIN'S LOG STARDATE 230018
Three days to go. Crew remain tense. Together we have decided to go on into the unknown as one body, for the benefit of all mankind. May this be a Leeson to us all.

Meanwhile media attention turned to the man who had broken the oldest bank in Britain. In the days after the crash, speculation as to Leeson's whereabouts rose to ridiculous proportions, with hordes of journalists speculating that he had fled on a false passport carrying suitcases of cash to locations as far apart as the jungles of Thailand and the forests of Canada by road, plane or on his luxury yacht named Lisa – the phantom yacht which sank mid-week taking the mythical Porsche with it. Even as his plane was landing in Frankfurt on Thursday, reporters mobbed a Leeson lookalike in Hong Kong.

While the rest of the world was looking for them, the Leesons were basking in the Malaysian sunshine. Nick and Lisa spent two days relaxing on sun loungers beside the hotel's two large swimming pools, reading and talking. They took a white-water river rafting trip at Beaufort in the hills near Kota Kinabalu; holiday snaps taken on a throwaway camera and published in the *Sun* newspaper showed Nick taking a tumble from the raft and floating in the river. They ate several meals in their room, but also dined at the hotel's seafood restaurant built on a peninsula, and at the seafood market, a fifteen-minute walk away, where customers select their meal from tanks of live fish.

Lisa remains adamant that the trip had been planned as part of Nick's twenty-eighth birthday celebrations; they had intended to go with friends, but because Nick was so stressed out they went on their own to talk things over. She insists that they had no idea he was the target of a global manhunt until the Monday evening when they strolled back into the hotel for a cup of tea. While she chose a packet of biscuits, Nick noticed a Barings headline on the front page of a local paper at the hotel kiosk. 'I was so shocked when I first saw the headline in the *Borneo Times* that I couldn't bring myself to pick up the paper,' Leeson reportedly told the *Sun*, adding that he had to ask Lisa to read the story to him. 'When I heard the bank was closing I just thought "Oh my God." My legs started shaking, it was like going into an exam. I knew Barings had lost a lot of money, but I never imagined they were on the brink of disaster.' Back in Singapore their apartment was already padlocked, following a raid by the Commercial Affairs Department which had seized documents and clothes.

For Nick Leeson the end was drawing nigh. On the Tuesday, wearing shorts, a white T-shirt, baseball cap and sun glasses, he showed up at the Royal Brunei Airlines office after checking out of the hotel at 7.40 that morning. Lisa who was with him wore a purple T-shirt and shorts. Leeson paid almost 4,000 ringit (about £1000) in cash for two tickets to Frankfurt, the only European-bound flight Royal Brunei had on offer for the next day.

There was nothing unusual about the transaction, except that it had been made in cash and the matter might have rested there, had Leeson not pointed out a mistake on the ticket, which had been issued in the name of 'Lesson'. It was 'Leeson' he stressed. The following day the two airline sales girls were reading the local paper when they spotted the photograph of the missing trader and his name. The local police were called, but seemed to attach little urgency to the tip-off. Reporters at the local newspaper, the *Sabah Daily Express*, however, immediately swung into action when they caught wind of the best scoop that had ever come their way. They alerted airport authorities and faxed their Thursday splash 'Barings Leeson escaped to KL?' to the British High Commission in Kuala Lumpur. The word was out.

The Leeson's left Malaysia at 9.15 a.m. on Wednesday morning on a 52-seater Royal Brunei Fokker Friendship. It was by an ironic twist of fate that 55 minutes later they arrived at Bandar Seri Bega-wan in Brunei, from where Barings' only hope of salvation had come. There they remained in transit for seven hours before leaving for Germany.

On Thursday, 2 March, as Dutch financial giant ING entered into exclusive talks to buy Barings, the search for Leeson came to an end. Exactly a week after he had disappeared, Nick and Lisa were detained by five German police officers as they funnelled off

Flight 535 in the cold Frankfurt dawn. Leeson who was wearing blue jeans and grey button-down shirt and carrying a paperback thriller – Tom Clancy's *Without Remorse* – looked tanned but unshaven. Although the Leesons had been hoping to travel on to England, they put up no resistance to arrest, Nick reportedly offering himself to the police with the words, 'Yes, I'm the man you want.' By Thursday night Leeson was growing accustomed to his 12 ft by 8 ft cell in a Frankfurt jail where the maximum he could earn would be £3.50 a day as a cook or cleaner, if he behaved well, while Lisa made her way back towards England for a reunion with her family.

The news of Leeson's detention was greeted with guffaws and cheers at the Singapore futures exchange where he had made his ill-starred trades, while in England Leeson's younger sister Vicky used the *Watford Observer* to tell the world that her brother was: 'the nicest person on earth'.

Leeson's detention had brought one chapter of the saga to a close, but his own case, and the unravelling of exactly what had gone awry at Barings, had only just begun.

3 | The Heath Cult

'Are you hungry?'

From its inception, Baring Securities was stamped with the unmistakable hallmark of its founding father, Christopher Heath. His influence was all-pervasive, from the personalities and motivation of the young people he recruited, to the company's ethics and the culture and working environment he created. This influence was at its strongest during the Eighties when Heath was at the height of his power, but it was a foundation which was to prove difficult to tear up, even years after his departure, due to the large numbers of employees within Baring Securities who had been brought up in the broking world under his wing and maintained many of his views. The clash in attitude between Baring Brothers and Baring Securities which arose in the early Nineties epitomized a market-wide cultural rift between the conservative world of banking and the more opportunistic environment of broking, but at Baring Securities Heath had created a phenomenon verging on a personality cult, which amplified that cultural gap.

Christopher Heath was a veritable caricature of the Eighties super-broker; a Krug-drinking man who wore spit-polished brogues and immaculate suits, with the charm, wit and *joie de vivre* to live up to this image. He was a charismatic – some would say overbearing – character, whose presence was ubiquitous.

I first met him in June 1988 when he had flown into Tokyo from London for one of the most exciting and seminal days in Baring Securities' history: the firm's first day of trading on the Tokyo Stock Exchange. The office was buzzing with excitement. The salesmen and traders, all dressed in black tie for the occasion, were receiving order after congratulatory order from their clients; such a volume in fact that even those in the research department were roped in to man the telephones, which were ringing off their hooks, and to write sales tickets. Heath was in his element. He strode around the dealing room beaming, jacket off to reveal rolled-up sleeves and red braces, his brown eyes alert behind round glasses, patting people on the back and giving two thumbs up for every order that flooded in. These were qualities which I soon realized were always prevalent. Heath had a smile and a 'How are you?' for everyone, even the most recent recruits. He made casual enquiries about what everyone was working on, but made a particular effort to get to know those who were on the sharper end of the business. Aside from Ascot, it was in the dealing room, where he had started out himself, that he perhaps felt most at home.

Heath was the consummate salesman, 'You can never get a word in edgeways because he's always trying to sell you a job, a concept, a block of shares, a horse,' a Barings salesman said to me soon after I joined the firm. He had a keen nose for a good money-spinner and was always willing to take a punt on anything he thought was a winner. 'Christopher was driven by financial interest, but more than that he had a keen and instinctive feel for money-making opportunities, which he promoted with great energy and gusto,' says Andrew Baylis, Deputy Chairman of Baring Securities Ltd from 1984 to 1992. 'He is not the world's most searing intellect, but he does have a tremendous instinct for something of potential. He brought a wonderful enthusiasm to [the business] and a willingness to take risks and back his own judgment.'

His attitude to business was reflected in his personal life. Heath was an avid horse lover, owning a string of racehorses himself and sometimes even managing to persuade traders to invest in legs of various fillies; he bought early into the bulk warehouse wine business in the UK through Majestic Wine Warehouses and invested in a diverse series of other ventures from party planning to a firm which brought the Sequence system of fast-changing perimeter advertising placards to Britain's football grounds. Naturally, he had to look for opportunities to invest the substantial amounts of money he made as Managing Director of Baring Securities. A stream of new business ideas came from his insatiably chatty approach to air travel. During the course of the many miles he flew on behalf of Barings he would always grill his neighbouring passengers for information and suggestions, a habit that perhaps made him a less than ideal partner for long international flights in many travellers' minds.

A cartoon typifying these characteristics, and commonly assumed to be Heath, was chosen in the early days of the company's history to decorate the walls of the Baring Securities' offices in London and Tokyo, no doubt because of its likeness. It portrayed a portly, bespectacled man striding down a condo-lined beach in a T-shirt emblazoned with the maxim: BUY LOW, SELL HIGH. This simplistic message could easily have been regarded as Heath's chosen company motto.

Because of its auspicious connotations in Chinese numerology, 1988 was deemed a good year to begin TSE trading. At the exhortation of one of the Chinese equity saleswomen, all members of staff were obliged to reinforce that luck by partaking of a traditional suckling pig, complete with cherry eyes and all the trimmings, set out on a plastic sheet on a conference room table. Luck was certainly in that day: Baring Securities achieved the record for the highest volume of shares ever traded by any securities firm on its first day of trading on the TSE, but it was evident that the firm's success had more to do with the original foresight of Baring Brothers in seeking a Far Eastern investment, and Christopher Heath's talent at selling that concept, than anything to do with Chinese superstition.

Heath had joined forces with Baring Brothers four years before my arrival in Tokyo during a period when the City of London was launching headlong into the twentieth century and traditional merchant banks such as Barings were being given the opportunity to transform themselves.

In 1984 Baring Brothers & Co. Ltd, seemed set for genteel obscurity. The original bank, nearly 250 years old was well regarded. It had a solid fund-management arm and a good line in advising eminent international clients like the World Bank, Pirelli, Inchcape, Blue Circle, Allied Lyons and the Saudi royal family.

Otherwise, there was little except respectability to show for two centuries of banking tradition. Its corporate finance team, for instance, though able to boast a few successes, seemed outstripped by the leading London houses. Although Barings could hold its head up among other merchant banks, it was not the largest, and it was dwarfed by British clearing banks like National Westminster or Barclays. It was in short exactly the sort of family-run business which Big Bang – the deregulation of the UK's financial industry – looming on the horizon in 1986, seemed set to sweep away.

'In the early to mid-Eighties, the pressure was building,' explains a Baring Brothers executive. 'Barings' UK corporate finance business was deteriorating, losing clients. The US houses were making a tremendous play for the UK corporate market and some of the British houses like Morgan Grenfell and Warburgs were aggressively attacking the client bases of more sleepy institutions like Barings. In the lead-up to the purchase of Henderson Crosthwaite (Far East), Barings hadn't grasped the fact that corporate finance was changing. It wasn't a question of knowing the yellow pages backwards any more. A proactive, entrepreneurial approach to deals was required.'

Big Bang – so-called because it offered the City a chance to re-invent itself – promised a wholesale deregulation of London's financial markets and the chance for banks like Barings to shake themselves awake and move forward in time. Before Big Bang, Barings and other merchant banks were dubbed 'issuing houses' because they issued securities but couldn't trade or distribute them and they maintained a haughty aloofness from the trading floor. Big Bang promised them the sudden opportunity to broaden the range of services they could offer by buying jobbers (market-makers) and brokers, the wholesalers and retailers of the London stock exchange where gilts and shares were transacted; in theory the chance to develop into modern investment banks on the American model. At the time, the London press made a telling distinction between the patrician 'gentlemen' of the merchant banks, who inhabited the more elitist world of corporate finance and money management, and the 'players' of the brokerage firms, who dabbled in the world of trading. The idea was that the new British conglomerates would develop a synthesis of these two worlds. Ultimately what transpired however, was that in many cases the gentlemen and the players never saw eye to eye.

In the run up to Big Bang, as the opportunities grew more apparent, the City saw a frenzied scramble by the larger-capitalized banks – both British and foreign – to find partners among existing broking and jobbing firms. From late 1983 there was a flurry of matchmaking: Citicorp formed a triple alliance with Scrimgeour Kemp-Gee and Vickers Da Costa, Kleinwort Benson paired up with Grievson Grant, and Barclays formed a liaison with de Zoete and Wedd Durlacher Mordaunt. Some of the partners in hasty engagements such as these were subsequently to prove disastrous bedfellows – where firms had married in haste and would be forced to repent at their leisure – but at the time marriage was the thing to do. Having had their own overtures to Cazenove rejected, Baring Brothers had been making money from acting as matchmaker for unions between other institutions. Nonetheless, they were still scouting for a suitable partner for themselves when on to the floor waltzed their perfect match: Christopher Heath.

When the executives of Baring Brothers met Christopher Heath in 1984, he had already been working in the City for fifteen years, having left ICI in 1969 to join a traditional English stockbroking partnership, George Henderson & Co. (later part of Henderson Crosthwaite & Co.) which was involved with both private client and institutional broking. At Henderson's, Heath was thrown in at the deep end, but quickly learnt the ropes of the brokerage business under the tutelage of Denis Russell, formerly a senior partner at Henderson's, and with the aid of a book called *Beginners Please*, the gentlemanly beginner's guide to stockbroking which has become a City classic.

In 1974, when the UK market was in a very bleak state, Heath shared a flat with James Nelson who had been following the Japanese market as a fund manager for the investment firm Foreign and Colonial. Nelson encouraged Heath to take a look at Japan himself and, after a late-night pep talk in which Nelson gave him five reasons why he should invest there (namely, inflation had fallen, GNP was soaring, the yen was growing stronger, the Japanese workforce was hard-working and highly educated and Japan was emerging as a nation with strong product leadership, particularly in electronics and autos), Heath began to buy up the only three UK-quoted, UK-registered Japanese investment trusts which were then available, for his institutional clients. At the time, the trusts traded at a huge discount (almost 65 per cent) to the value of the shares held in them, because of the cautious outlook for Japan following the first OPEC oil crisis, but by May of the following year they were all on small premiums. The big break came for Heath when one of the three investment trust firms whose funds he had been recommending approached him to assist them in the placing of units of a new issue. Despite the last-minute withdrawal of the firm's original brokers, Heath and his team placed 25 per cent of the issue (1.25 million shares at 139 pence per share) on their own.

In the wake of his initial success, Heath became an avid follower of the market and in February 1976 went on his first visit to Japan at the invitation of Nomura. Over the next few years he went to Japan regularly, visiting Japanese companies, writing up research reports, and coming back via Hong Kong where he began to establish relationships with international investment management companies operating there, such as Jardine Fleming, GT and Henderson Baring (no relation to Henderson Crosthwaite). Over the next few years Henderson Crosthwaite's and particularly Heath's reputation and business grew with the success of his investment recommendations and the firm's capacity to fill buy and sell orders for Hong Kong clients on the OTC market in London when the Japanese market was closed.

Heath's drive to make money by helping foreigners to buy and sell Japanese shares may in part have stemmed from his personal life. His father, Lieutenant-General Sir Lewis Macclesfield Heath, and his New Zealand-born mother, Katherine, were trapped in Singapore on their way to a Middle East posting in 1941. When the island fell to the Japanese, the General and his wife were taken prisoners of war. The Heaths spent the rest of the war in captivity in Changi, now the site of Singapore's international airport, where their baby daughter was born and subsequently died. In 1946 General Heath retired and the couple moved to Kenya where, later that year, Christopher was born.

In November of 1983 Heath was asked to a lunch in the stately Baring Brothers offices at Bishopsgate hosted by John Dare and Michael Baring (both directors) to discuss the fledgling Japanese warrant bond market. Baring Brothers had been involved in the placement of new warrant bond issues and wanted to know more about the trading of the warrant paper once it had been separated from the bond part of the package; how the warrants moved; and what kind of investors bought them.

During the course of that lunch Heath was asked what Henderson Crosthwaite intended to do in Big Bang. By that time he was one of thirty-one partners in the firm which was producing over 60 per cent of its profits from its Far Eastern activities, for which Heath had been awarded his partnership and as such had a voting right in the firm's future.

Six weeks after the lunch, at the beginning of 1984, Baring Brothers formally approached Heath with an offer to set up a new brokerage firm under Barings' name, staffed by the core of Heath's team at Henderson Crosthwaite & Co. for the small sum of £6 million. In May a deal was struck to establish a specialist Asian stockbroking firm called Baring Far East Securities. (It was renamed Baring Securities in 1986.) The new subsidiary was to be completely autonomous, with separate management and offices. In order to give the employees a direct interest in the annual results of the firm, it was to retain 50 per cent of its profits before tax, after a capital charge, for distribution amongst its staff, with the other 50 per cent going to Baring Brothers & Co., its parent.

That early independence was to prove critical to Baring Securities' success. Post-Big Bang, many liaisons fell apart as a result of a lack of understanding between the broking and banking sides of the business and because the broking arms proved to be costly partners. Most of the previously flourishing brokers were run into the ground by the banks that bought them. An analyst at Barclays de Zoete Wedd estimated that up to 1991 over £1.5 billion in goodwill was paid by banks acquiring brokers in London and that the majority were investments which, by the early Nineties, showed scarcely any return. Most were businesses which concentrated on the saturated, over-broked markets of the UK and Europe, and the acquisition of Henderson Crosthwaite (Far East) was in that light a progressive move on the part of Baring Brothers.

The key element in the success of the match was the fact that The Brothers (as they were commonly called) and Securities had based their marriage on an agreement that they wouldn't share the same bed. Both the banking and the broking side of the business were in accord on this point. Andrew Tuckey, then Chairman of Baring Brothers & Co., noted in an interview with *The Sunday Times* in 1991 that conventional wisdom around the time of Big Bang was that merchant banks had to become 'integrated houses', combining broking and banking services. 'We were involved in some of the sales of brokerships. We weren't convinced the cultures were compatible enough and we were horrified at the prices.'

Heath agreed with Tuckey's view. 'We had an environment in which we could build the business, in that we were totally independent of Baring Brothers, so we had no daily cultural battle to fight, which a lot of other firms had after Big Bang when they tried to weld a whole lot of people who were not suited to working together,' he says a decade later, reflecting on those early years. 'The merchant banking culture and the broking culture are very different at the end of the day. The relationship I had with Andrew Tuckey and John Dare in those days was extremely good. It was a dialogue which one felt very comfortable with and one felt them there in the background as very supportive partners, rather than an interfering force.'

Heath started out with a team of only fifteen, ten of whom were based in the London head office and five in the new representative office in Tokyo, specializing in Japanese equities and warrants. In Tokyo offices the firm began in humble surroundings; the first office was in an annexe of the petfood department of Dodwells and clients had to wade through stacks of dog and cat food on their way to receive investment advice. Shortly afterwards they moved to offices near the Okura hotel, and the young team of five would bring their swimsuits and sun cream to work in the morning on sunny days, and once they had written up and faxed out the morning news and recommendations to clients, they would retire to the swimming pool in the Okura. This relaxed approach to business was swiftly brought to a halt when the orders started flowing.

The founding members of Baring Far East Securities – Andrew Baylis, John Bonfield, Christopher Derricott, Andrew Fraser, Richard Greer, Diarmaid Kelly, Alex Murray, Roy Johnson, and Colin Ring – had all been at Henderson Crosthwaite together. Six of the original team (Derricott, Fraser, Greer, Kelly, Murray and Johnson) still remained at Barings a decade later. Christopher Heath was appointed Managing Director of BFES and Andrew Baylis, John Bonfield, Andrew Fraser, Richard Greer and Colin Ring were Executive Directors. John Dare, a director of Baring Brothers & Co. Ltd was appointed non-executive Chairman, while Andrew Tuckey, Michael Baring and John McLaren, also from Baring Brothers, were non-executive directors.

In the early years of Baring Securities the senior management from Henderson Crosthwaite were viewed as a very tight-knit group. Heath and Kelly had both attended Ampleforth College, a Catholic public school in Yorkshire, and the myth that most of the founding directors were Catholic spread to the extent that this governing group were eventually nicknamed the 'Catholic Mafia'. It was even rumoured that the directors exercised a deliberate policy of recruiting old boys and Catholics. The perception persisted well into the late Eighties, when a new salesman was overheard saying to a Chinese colleague:

'I'm a Catholic, Nicola's a Catholic, Christopher's a Catholic, so what are you?'

'It begins with C,' she replied, 'but the C stands for Communist.'

Heath is amused by such nonsense. 'Diarmaid [Kelly] was at Ampleforth many years after me and certainly wasn't a church-going Catholic, Andrew Baylis and [Andrew] Fraser certainly weren't Catholics, and Richard Greer was very much Protestant – the son of a Bishop. The only common line between the original partners was that we were all "only" children, which was a strange thing.'

When Heath set up Baring Securities, he brought with him a core of like-minded individuals who were experts in the Japanese markets. Over the years they were joined by a variety of others: employees who had worked their way up through the back office, impressionable graduates, externally hired professional securities staff, the occasional nepotistically appointed relation (sometimes those of a client), and a handful of 'larger-than-life' and slightly incongruous characters.

It was clear during the Eighties, that, although there was never a specific intention to establish such a hiring policy, many of Baring Securities' employees came from the same mould as Heath. Those taking ultimate hiring decisions sought personality, self-assuredness and drive, on the basis that in the broking business the latter qualities often outweighed education, professional experience or management expertise. The most significant of these qualities, 'drive', being, in the financial world, most commonly and crudely associated with money. This was to prove both a strength and a weakness in the culture which developed.

Heath believed in interviewing potential employees himself whenever possible, particularly if they were being recruited to work in the sales or research departments, but even if they were being recruited as back office functionaries or receptionists. Once, when questioned about the latter, he replied 'Certainly. They are the first impression anyone gets of an office.' Securities' initial success can in large part be attributed to this hands-on hiring policy.

In hiring sales staff and traders, Heath was always keen to ensure that they had a healthy appetite for money-making opportunities, both personal and corporate. When asked why you wanted to join Barings or go into the broking business, there was only one correct answer. To say that you were looking for job satisfaction, had a desire for responsibility, an ambition for authority, or wanted to provide a professional service to the clients – qualities which Heath took as a given – did not wash. The best answer was that you wanted money, the more the better. This, of course, was a safe answer for anyone in the City – broking is seldom associated with the enhancement of spirituality – but in Heath's world, recognition of that fact was of paramount importance. One of Heath's favourite interview questions was: 'Are you hungry?' Many candidates, imagining that they were about to get a free lunch on the company said 'yes', inadvertently giving the correct answer.

Certain employees epitomized the Heath philosophy better than others. Sales staff, particularly in overseas branches, not only began their frenzied fact-gathering, fact-faxing, telephone-monopolized day at chronically early hours, but also spent most of their free time with clients. It is a conventional British broking ethic to inextricably associate entertainment with the job, the tradition of long boozy lunches in the old days of the City having now been replaced with mineral water at lunchtime and long nights out on the town, particularly in Asia. Most felt that Heath and other senior managers expected them – and they were willing – to entertain clients both at lunchtime *and* in the evenings, often into the small hours of the morning, while still sustaining their early-morning starts and long office hours. Weekends too were given up to client entertainment, be it skiing or golf, a trip to Disneyland or a football game – whatever the client wanted. This 24-hour service fostered excellent business relationships and nurtured close friendships as many of the clients at that time were young and single like their brokers and simply wanted to go out and have fun.

Salesmen from the head office in London visiting Asian offices, particularly Japan, with their clients, amply demonstrated this party ethos. One London salesman and his client enjoyed a typically vibrant evening in a Japanese *robotayaki* restaurant called Sendagaya, in the Roppongi district of Tokyo, known locally as the 'shouting' restaurant because the chefs yell out the dishes as they serve them to diners. The couple were the last to leave the restaurant that evening and as the staff prepared to close up, the salesman went to collect his jacket which he had hung on a hook by the door. However, the only navy jacket left was three sizes too small. The disappearance of his own jacket was not a considerable problem in itself, but he had foolishly left his wallet, passport and air ticket for his flight home the next morning in the jacket when he hung it up. It was perhaps not surprising in the consumer-conscious Eighties that, as he flew around the office hungover and in a state of panic the next morning, the item he seemed most concerned about losing was his new Platinum American Express card. His jacket was mercifully returned to the reception desk at the eleventh hour before his departure by a middle-aged Japanese housewife. As was usual in Japan at that time, everything was in place, including the Amex card. The only thing out of place was the knot which had been tied in the left arm of the jacket. The housewife quickly scuttled off as the salesman inspected it, finding to his horror that the borrower had been so considerate about keeping his taxi clean the previous night that he had thrown up into the sleeve of what he thought was his own jacket.

It was a common joke that while the sales staff were out enjoying themselves, those in the research department were beavering away in the office. It was not unusual for analysts to give up their weekends or work through the night to ensure that research reports arrived complete and fully edited on a client's desk in London by Monday morning. The research department was often still buzzing at ten o'clock in the evening. 'We had a good team of people who were dedicated to building up the business and who were very client-oriented in terms of servicing the institutional clients,' says Heath. 'We never believed that the world owed us a living; the client wanted to do business and it was up to us to go to him. We didn't take the Baring Brothers' attitude which was "You can look us up in the telephone directory." We were dead hungry and got out there because the only way we were going to cut into what was a very competitive environment was by being thoroughly professional, having very high quality research and very good salesmen to put that message across.'

On days when clients were in town, the young, foreign staff in the Tokyo office were asked to go and collect them from the lobbies of their hotels and escort them back to their meetings in Baring Securities' offices. This was preceded by vigorous questioning from the Branch Manager, Richard Greer, to ensure that they were fully clued-up on market matters so as not to make fools of themselves or Barings. 'Have you read your daily news? What happened to the dollar this morning? Did you see the Bank of Japan statement . . . ?'

The young employees who performed this task, myself included, were predominantly women, and we were expected to dress up for the occasion. Due to the obvious chauvinistic connotations of this escort service and the rather fine line it drew between providing an attentive service for the clients and sexual discrimination, we sometimes resented management for putting us in this position. However, we made light of it by joking that the management would actually have preferred to have dressed us up in uniform and called us the Baring Bimbettes, but didn't dare push their luck that far.

Whether the service was actually appreciated by the clients remains in question. Jet-lagged and tired after long international flights, clients on some mornings might have preferred to doze in the back of the chauffeur-driven car, rather than have a young, enthusiastic broker rapping to them about the market, but the company was renowned for always offering more than was required. The service epitomized the 'human face' of the firm, which separated Barings from the more clinical US brokers or the stuffier British houses and it reflected management's genuine expectation that we would all do our best to get business.

At Barings the client (who was *never* referred to as a *customer*) was omnipotent. In Tokyo, the Five Commandments were hung on the noticeboard – only partly in jest:

1. The client is the most important person ever in this office.
2. The client does not depend on us; we depend on the client.
3. The client is not the nuisance of our work; he is the mainframe of it. We are not doing him a favour for having him; he is doing us a favour by giving us the opportunity to have him.
4. The client is not someone to argue or match wits with. Nobody ever wins an argument with the client.
5. The client is the person who brings us the bonus and it is our job to give him anything and everything he wants.

Baring Securities' clients enjoyed being right, but equally they appreciated the high level and personal nature of the service that the company offered them. 'You had to speak to Barings,' recalls a British fund manager. 'They were the biggest foreign house in the bull market and the most visible agency broker in Japan. Barings' opinions on things, for example the Osaka redevelopment story, could influence stock prices. It was the only brokerage house on the foreign side that the large Japanese investors listened to. They were good stockbrokers and knew what they were talking about. The main reason I spoke to them was because of the sales people there, and it still is. They were good, professional and also great fun. When they entertained you, they entertained you royally. There was no expense spared. They used to take us out for weird and wonderful lunches and dinners for which Barings is famous, but it was never a substitute for the professionalism of the service.'

The fun that Baring Securities brought to client relationships, combined with good salesmanship and high quality research, brought in a steady and lasting flow of business. Barings did not always offer the best prices, but they offered service with a difference. 'They were dealing with an organization that was in a sense an entrepreneurial, vibrant, young company which had gone out and found itself an extraordinary franchise in the Orient and emerging markets,' recalls Andrew Baylis. 'People respected it and liked dealing with it. It offered a professional service and one which reflected the markets it had grown up in. Barings was perceived as having a different character from the others. It developed a tremendous client loyalty.'

The other factor underpinning the Baring Securities culture during the Eighties was the presence of a number of 'larger-than-life' personalities in the firm. An enlivening and amusing by-product of Heath's preference for 'personality' was the consideration of a variety of candidates who came with a liberal sprinkling of what one might best describe as zaniness. If you included fortune-telling among the talents listed on your curriculum vitae, or had climbed the highest mountain, fought with tigers or been a trapeze artist, you were definitely in with the chance of an interview. This both attracted client interest and stimulated an alternative approach to what can be a humdrum business.

One former analyst at Barings, a geologist, was initially unsuccessful in his application. He too had been asked the hungry question in interview and, despite having missed his lunch and fancying a sandwich, recognized a cliché when he saw one and had said something like 'I can do without that', a response which obviously hadn't gone down particularly well. When the rejection letter came he called Heath to question it. Heath asked him to recount ten reasons why he should have been hired, but transferred the call to the office-wide tannoy system prior to the candidate replying. At the end of the geologist's soliloquy, Heath called out of his office for a vote on the performance, upon which he received a resounding thumbs up and promptly hired the candidate on the spot.

One candidate was offered an interview purely on the basis that on his CV, under summer vacation experience, he had written: 'Stacking shelves at Tesco, occasionally unsupervised'. The interviewers simply wished to see whether this was what they perceived to be evidence of an excellent sense of humour, or merely an indication of stupidity.

Another infamous example was a female analyst who, before she joined Barings, had unwittingly found herself dealing with religious propaganda for a language school in the south of Japan. Her application letter opened with the lines: 'Dear Sir, I'm desperate. I'm working for the Moonies and I need rescuing. Please help me out . . .'

This off-the-wall approach frequently paid dividends in terms of motivation, initiative and the fostering of good client relationships, but it had other by-products. The company encouraged its employees to pursue their interests, which they did zealously, spending a large proportion of their time climbing mountains and diving off wrecks. This produced a wealth of wonderful stories, but meant that there was no guarantee of the high productivity rates expected during working hours. For instance, the geologist, who performed excellently as a researcher, wound up getting delayed while crossing the Taklamakan Desert and turned up for work two weeks late armed with a battalion of photographs, but with a dulled appetite for his job. Eventually he broke free from the shackles of the business, having decided that he had more worthwhile things to do with his life.

More traditional candidates also had their hiccups. The company certainly didn't get what it was expecting when a new salesman turned up for his first day in the office. The Saturday night before his new job started, he went out celebrating and fell over whilst drunk, smashing his front teeth out on a pavement curbstone. The problem was compounded the following day when, having been up most of the night in the hospital, he fell asleep while having a haircut to be awoken with quarter-inch stubble on his head. The combination of his puffed up face and crew cut gave him the appearance of a National Front leader who had been kicked in the face with a Doc Marten. His face was so severely swollen and his head so brutally shorn that he was almost unrecognizable to those who had interviewed him; he certainly bore no resemblance to the smart professional whose appearance had contributed to his being appointed as one of the firm's senior salesmen in the Far East.

Management at Baring Securities demonstrated a similar level of forward thinking in their willingness to try out the latest in recruitment techniques. One of Heath's inspirational flashes was the introduction of handwriting tests as a form of candidate assessment; handwriting samples from all interviewees were couriered to Switzerland for testing. These tests proved remarkably successful, but not in the way that had been anticipated. Those responsible for recruitment soon ascertained that there was a remarkable consistency between low handwriting scores and a highly rated performance by the candidate in interview, consequently not everyone was as convinced of the efficacy of these tests as Heath. Matters finally came to a head when Heath hired an individual who had scored highly on the graphology test but had been roundly rejected by all who had interviewed him in person. The individual proved to be a disastrous recruit and Heath agreed to put an end to the tests.

The overall effect of this hiring policy was to create a group of people with very varied talents, a situation which was to persist throughout the life of the company. Even after the bank's crash, a new recruit from a US investment bank commented that whereas at his previous firm all the employees had displayed a similar standard of motivation and capability, 'at Barings there are people who are absolutely brilliant in their fields and some with lumps of coal for brains'.

Once on board at Barings a new recruit was, as Christopher Heath had been in his own time and as many in the broking world are, 'thrown in at the deep end' if he or she had no prior experience. There are of course both advantages and disadvantages to learning on the job; people are forced to learn quickly in order to keep up, but such informal training naturally requires constant supervision from more experienced staff to avoid costly mistakes.

While the culture at Baring Securities encouraged initiative, enthusiasm and individualism among the employees, what it lacked was the formality and tradition which had been established over a much longer period at Baring Brothers. In the nineteenth century Baring Brothers spent an inordinate amount of time training people and schooling them in a homogeneous culture. Recruits were apprenticed at firms in foreign capitals and passed through a period of protracted socialization before being elevated to positions of responsibility. This process was speeded up in the twentieth century, but a period of initiation was still a prerequisite before becoming a practising officer of the bank. A Baring Brothers executive who joined the bank in the Seventies recalls how he and other Oxbridge graduates began in the post room opening the mail and spent the following six months visiting each department in the bank. In addition to the internal training course, they were also taught law, economics and accountancy by a professor from the London School of Economics. 'In those days Barings was a venerable, staid, old-fashioned place with a strong public school and Oxbridge ethos,' he recalls.

If the stiff corporate bankers at Baring Brothers represented a straight-laced public school where everyone swatted for their A-levels and got into Oxford, the securities side of the business seemed at times like a rowdy grammar over which the Branch Manager in Tokyo presided like a young, well-meaning but rather harried headmaster. Whenever Christopher Heath was coming into town, he would fly into a frenzy: 'I want all these desks tidied up by tomorrow. And I want all of you on the phone, even in research. I don't care who you call, call your mother, but everyone must be on the phone. Just look busy.' Tired of such chastisement, on one of these occasions one of the salesmen deliberately made a point of letting Heath catch him reading the paper at his desk just as the market was opening. 'Why are you reading the paper? Get on the phone,' shouted Heath. 'I want to see you writing tickets.'

Such an approach merely indicated management's concern to keep the staff on their toes, but it was occasionally taken to a level which appeared pedantic. For instance, new graduates in the London office's research department were given regular spelling tests by senior managers, with words such as 'rhodedendrum' and 'diohrrea' on the list.

As in all brokerage houses, the money culture was firmly entrenched throughout all offices and departments in the company and was driven home constantly by such comments as: 'If you don't get this finished in time, your bonus will be cut.' The bonus was considered the ultimate stick and the ultimate carrot and instilled a concern for remuneration in even the most puritanical individual.

In direct contradiction to the more established, orderly environment of Baring Brothers, the dealing room at Baring Securities frequently descended into boyish chaos. Pranks were played by members of staff of all ages and positions. One of the directors who went for his morning constitutional during market hours had his inattentiveness pointed out to him very sharply by a young equity trader. He literally caught him with his pants down by throwing a bucket of water over him as he sat in the cubicle reading his *Financial Times*. Such acts were fully supported by all in the dealing room and considered a form of rough justice. Nevertheless, they invited swift retribution, which, in this particular case, took the form of the trader being bound to an office chair with Sellotape and left in the glass-walled elevator where he rode up and down, bound and gagged, until rescued by a benevolent employee from a neighbouring office.

Such high jinks didn't always start off on the moral high-ground.

Sometimes they were merely the result of a combination of boister-
ousness and stress that manifested itself in such childish pranks as
water-pistol fights between the trading and research departments.
Although inherently silly, these school-room antics demonstrated
the excellent morale amongst the employees, who felt very much
part of a family, rather than just a company.

The most senior members of staff, including Heath, nurtured
and relished the spirit of fun that prevailed within Securities. A
young equity trader who was being posted out to Tokyo from
London was told that he had to have a full medical before he went
to Japan, AIDS test included. He was delighted when a very pretty
nurse walked into the boardroom, asked him to strip off and began
to examine his particulars. His excitement rose apace when she
began to remove her own clothes. It was only when his colleagues
burst through the door wielding a camera as the strippergram was
giving the hernia test that he realized management had had the last
laugh. The photos of the medical were later blown up to life-size
and displayed in the dealing room.

Not surprisingly in small offices where the average age worldwide
was still well below thirty, staff members formed a tight-knit group,
even at a social level. When I joined the Tokyo office in 1988
there were only sixty employees, of which less than a fifth were
non-Japanese and whose average age was only about twenty-six.
After long working days of eleven or twelve hours, we would go
out together in a pack to the wealth of bars and restaurants which
Tokyo offered. Weekends were also spent with office colleagues
(and clients who were friends) at one of the three holiday houses
rented by the firm for the staff's and clients' enjoyment, which
were located by the beach, a skiing resort and in an *onsen* (hot-
spring) town respectively. These houses were particularly appreciated by the Japanese staff whose remuneration packages were lower
than those of the ex-pats. Tokyo set a pattern for other offices in the
Far East. In Hong Kong and Singapore, for instance, the company
provided yachts and junks for the staff's and clients' enjoyment,
with speed-boats for water skiing; in some cases they also paid for
membership of health clubs. The youthful team spirit born in
Tokyo and London became a tradition that was continued as Baring

Securities opened other offices around Asia. The fact that the firm's staff got on so well together and were like-minded created a productive and highly enjoyable working environment.

The identification of work colleagues with family members was reinforced by Christopher Heath, whose presence suggested that of head of the family. He and other senior members of staff took a close interest in the personal welfare of their staff. Personal touches extended to details like the giving of flowers, champagne or gifts to members of staff on occasions such as engagements, and to senior staff members attending the weddings of juniors. New arrivals in Asia would be sent a copy of a local guidebook and a personal note from the Branch Manager welcoming them, as would all visiting clients. The fraternal atmosphere fostered strong friendships amongst colleagues and a high degree of personal, rather than just financial, support at all levels that made the world of difference, especially to staff posted overseas. Visitors and new arrivals frequently commented on the warmth of their reception and the intimacy of the environment within Baring Securities' overseas offices. 'The character and temperament of those involved was to encourage close personal ties and loyalties – it was old-fashioned and paternalistic,' says Andrew Baylis, Deputy Managing Director of Baring Securities Ltd from 1984 to 1992. 'The group was closely linked and pulling together because of the sort of people they were, in comparison with organizations run on objective, detached, authoritarian guidelines.'

The general response from employees to this environment was a feeling of strong respect and loyalty to Christopher Heath and other senior managers, which in turn fostered a feeling of personal responsibility towards Baring Securities.

On the back of bullish markets in the Eighties and the commitment of the company's employees, profits flowed ever more quickly through Baring Securities' doors. This led to a dramatic expansion of both the number of employees and the company's network, but naturally also engendered a breakdown of the family feeling previously enjoyed. The change was most noticeable in the attitudes of the employees; there was a decline in personal loyalty and responsibility which was largely replaced by commitment of a more professional nature, but in the worst cases it made room for complacency and even the abuse of the generosity which the company had previously shown.

4 | The Tail Begins to Wag

'We were the cheeky upstart, the cuckoo in the nest.'
ANDREW BAYLIS

In the five years after Christopher Heath and his team set up Baring Securities, Japan underwent a period of extraordinary economic growth. Between February 1985 and February 1988 the value of the yen more than doubled against the dollar; people expected the economy to slip into recession, but suddenly Japan's domestic demand boomed and, far from slumping, the economy expanded at its fastest rate for six years with corporate profits growing lustily. Not even Black Monday, the world stock market crash in October 1987, could derail Japan; its market fell less than that of any other country and recovered far faster. By 1988 Japan had become the world's largest creditor nation; it could boast the world's biggest stock market, the world's biggest stockbrokers, the best-capitalized financial institutions and the richest corporations. Just one company listed on the Tokyo Stock Exchange for instance, Nippon Telephone and Telegraph Corp. (NTT), was worth more than all of the stocks listed on the West German and Hong Kong stock markets combined. The country's economic resilience and buying ability led people to think that Japan would become an invincible global superpower.

As such, Japan was an amazing place to live in the Eighties, especially for those in their twenties. In comparison with the more trying economic environments of the US and UK, Japan offered a carefree, fun environment because, seemingly overnight, the whole nation had more money in their pockets than they had ever dreamt of. The general level of wealth created by the economic bubble filtered down to all levels of Japanese society including those in their teens and twenties, creating a massively consumer conscious group of people who loved to shop, to travel and to party.

The bubble economy and resulting demand for opportunities to spend money spawned the creation of a plethora of wacky bars, nightclubs and restaurants, many of which were financed by money that would otherwise have been paid out in corporate tax. The explosion and rapid turnover of such venues had been witnessed in other capital cities in other eras, such as New York in the Seventies, but in Tokyo it was accompanied by a unique level of expenditure which extended not only to state-of-the-art sound systems and interior design, but the construction of entirely new buildings by some of the world's leading contemporary architects merely to house a restaurant or club. You could enjoy a beer in the Asahi Beer Hall designed by Phillippe Starck to resemble a glass of stout with the froth on top (though it looks more like a golden flame), have a cocktail in a Roppongi bar called Solemn which was decorated to resemble a Bedouin tent with white drapery, sand on the floor, Middle Eastern music and a golden camel at its door, or in Blue where baby sharks hunted up and down in a tank running along one wall. Gold, a vast, five-storey warehouse nightclub with vending machines for alcoholic drinks, opened on the waterfront in Tokyo; it held regular invitation theme party nights and attracted a zany crowd of stylish young Japanese who sported the wildest of outfits.

The money spent on promoting these ludicrously expensive ventures was equally absurd. The British architect Nigel Coates designed the Wall building, in Nishi Azabu, Tokyo, to house a restaurant, club and bar in 1990. On the opening night of the club, a fire-engine red Maserati Spyder that was parked out front with a giant white ribbon tied round its bonnet, was the first prize in a raffle.

Japan's strong economic growth, tight labour markets, increasing domestic demand and expanding domestic liquidity sent the Japanese stock market shooting up. In the five years after Heath set up Baring Securities, the Tokyo stock market tripled, briefly outstripping Wall Street in size.

Japan had been making painfully slow, but steady, paces towards liberalization and internationalization of its securities markets. One of the changes introduced by a Ministry of Finance paper was the extension of membership of the Tokyo Stock Exchange in 1986 to ten more firms, of which, for the first time, six were foreigners. In September 1986 Baring Securities achieved branch office status and in 1988 was admitted to the membership of the Exchange.

The strength of the Tokyo stock market alone in the mid-Eighties was enough to ensure profitability for any well-positioned participant. Baring Securities showed massive profits within the first two years of its existence and was to capitalize on this early success throughout the Eighties. The firm's success stemmed not simply from the fact that it had got into Japan early, however, but because Baring Securities had another edge there: mastery of the rather obscure, but rapidly expanding market in Japanese equity warrants.

Japanese companies began to issue warrant bonds in the early Eighties because they provided them with a cheap source of funds. In order that those companies could pay much lower interest on the bonds that they issued, warrants were attached to each bond as a 'sweetener' to investors. The warrant allowed investors to buy shares in the company of the bond issuer, at a set price and over a predetermined period, usually between three and five years. On exercise the warrants would raise sufficient funds to repay the debt, removing the need to repay the bond.

The warrants were traded separately from the bonds and the underlying shares, forming a highly leveraged options market on Japanese equities. Given the rapid growth in the Japanese economy and the accompanying boom in the share market, the issuers expected these warrant sweeteners to prove very popular and that the warrant bond issues would be a great success.

The issuance of these bonds came at a time when Japanese banks had excessive amounts of capital. Ironically, the Japanese banks bought vast quantities of these Japanese company bonds anyway (they always preferred to invest in Japanese, rather than foreign names), but without the warrants, the value of which was initially not appreciated by investors, most of whom concentrated on buying either bonds or shares.

It was only two or three years after the first warrant issues that mainstream equity investors started to appreciate the worth of these products for the exposure to the seemingly irrepressible Tokyo stock market which they offered, or the majority of brokers realized the money that could be made from dealing in the issues. By that time Baring Securities was well established as the leading market maker and distributor of these products. Realizing the market's potential, Heath had poached a fledgling team of warrant traders from Robert Fleming & Co., the first company to have established such a team when the market was in its embryonic stages. In this way he was able to capitalize on the boom which ensued. As Japanese companies continued to pursue cheap financing, the warrant bond market expanded dramatically in the mid to late Eighties. In the period 1985–1990 the total value of shares that could be created by these warrants exceeded US$150 billion, a figure equal to the capitalization of some smaller European stock markets.

In the 1980s there was no general forum for publishing these prices on news screens so that investors could check whether or not prices were fair relative to the underlying shares. Investors could only establish relative pricing by telephoning different market makers and comparing price quotations, which meant that prices were less transparent than if they had been publicly quoted on an exchange. This lack of transparency, combined with wide spreads between bids and offers and an underlying market that was enjoying one of the greatest economic booms of the twentieth century, enabled traders who commanded a strong position, by virtue of their customer base and market knowledge, to make enormous profits. Baring Securities made the utmost of this opportunity and its success in the Japanese warrant market accounted for the vast majority of its earnings from 1985 to 1989.

The staff of Baring Securities were, with good reason, especially proud of their success in this market, particularly those who were directly responsible for it. Trevor Sliwerski, one of the original recruits from Robert Fleming and a director of the firm, epitomized this better than anyone else and displayed such enthusiasm for warrants that visitors to his home were often impressed by the ability of even his children to quote warrant prices. At the height of the warrant market Sliwerski went on a ten-day trek in Nepal, during which he delighted in explaining the intricacies of the market to his fellow travellers. On his return to London, Sliwerski opened his *Financial Times* one morning to find that his holiday and market stories had been recounted in detail by one of these travellers who, unbeknownst to him, was a travel journalist for the paper. It was not until reading this article that he realized his passion for his work was such that he had talked of little else. The article delighted his colleagues in the dealing room who had to listen to his market tales day in, day out and teased him unmercifully about it.

Baring Securities' profitability in the Eighties was reflected in the way the firm treated its clients, whom it had always considered the mainstay of its business. Client entertainment had always been generous, but in the Eighties bull market, especially in Japan, it verged on the excessive. One particularly memorable example is the time Nick Faldo was flown in to play golf with four Barings employees and four clients. Each player had his photo taken with Faldo by a professional photographer and in addition to these individual portraits a calendar was made up including shots of all the participants.

Excess in the Eighties knew no bounds, especially to the Japanese. In London, one fund manager asked his Japanese broker to take him out to the Golden Nugget casino in Shaftesbury Avenue where the owners of local Chinese restaurants gamble with their takings. He added that he would like the broker to bring some money. The Japanese broker turned up with a box containing £10,000 in cash which he had procured from his company, looking forward to an evening at the tables. The fund manager promptly took the box from him and disappeared. He was spotted several weeks later driving round town in a second-hand Ferrari.

During this period Baring Securities showered its clients with gifts. In the late Eighties a salesman visiting the Tokyo office from London heard about the new bathroom gadgets which played the sound of a toilet flush – designed to save water in public toilets where Japanese women insist on flushing constantly – and decided to take a couple back as gifts for his clients. A strange gift, one might think, but the devices became such a rage among Barings' London-based clients that a request for more was sent out. The firm's financial analyst in Tokyo, a man who was an active member of the Young Conservatives and who had ambitions to pursue a career in politics, was most embarrassed at the possible ramifications of being confronted with forty of these devices in his luggage when he went back to the UK on a home visit.

Baring Securities staff were well rewarded for the part they had played in the firm's success and, in Asia particularly, used their generous remuneration to make the most of all the opportunities which life in the region offered. Encouraged by the considerably more materialistic and consumer-oriented environment of the East, the young ex-pats indulged themselves in foreign holidays and became the most avid of shoppers. Splashing out on first-class travel, four-star hotels and designer-label clothes became common-place and in the absence of the need for your own set of wheels in a country where public transport was so efficient, many people bought hifis at the cost of small cars. At the more imaginative end of the scale, a senior member of the Tokyo staff purchased a number of working Russian tanks that had been salvaged from the Gulf War and even put in a bid for a scud missile.

Such was the feeling of new-found wealth, in Japan generally as much as in Baring Securities, that at times it became difficult to keep the value of that money in perspective, particularly when living in a country where most goods cost at least three times the price they would in Europe or the US. I once went out to dinner in a restaurant called Cibreo in the funky new Nigel Coates-designed building in Nishi Azabu, Tokyo with a group of friends. We had enjoyed a meal and a fair few drinks when one of my friends ordered another bottle of wine at the cost of £500. As if this wasn't sufficient, he then went on to order another at £1,000, an excellent bottle of wine which, as it had not been allowed to breathe, and to the dismay of all who had partaken of it, was practically finished before it came into its element. Although amused at the time at this active lunacy, we at least had our wits sufficiently about us to make it clear that the wine, if consumed, would be paid for by the guy who had insisted on ordering it.

On another occasion one of the equity traders held a birthday party at his favourite Italian restaurant in Tokyo, Prego, attended by at least fifteen colleagues and a number of clients who were friends. Dom Perignon was served from eight in the evening until four in the morning and the evening spawned a new cocktail: a popular shot drink enjoyed in the bar called Shotguns, made of liquidized fresh fruit and Polish rectified spirit, was combined with champagne. This slammer concoction was christened Domperigun and has been immortalized on Prego's cocktail list.

The huge success of the Japanese business, particularly in warrants, provided fuel for growth into other emerging markets. Heath transformed Baring Securities within a few years from a tiny, Japan-specialist stockbroker into an organization of high repute in global emerging markets, a pace of growth which outstripped most of the foreign competition. From only fifteen employees at its inception in 1984, the company grew to a staff of over a thousand by 1991. Most of the initial expansion was in the Asia Pacific area; the Hong Kong office was set up in 1985 and within the space of a few years was complemented by offices in Singapore, Malaysia, Thailand, Taiwan, South Korea, Indonesia, the Philippines and Australia. Through the Eighties and into the early Nineties the lion's share of the profits were made from the broking and trading of Japanese products which underwrote the cost of the firm's rapid expansion programme.

Baring Securities' profitability was evident in the quality of its offices, which became increasingly luxurious, though they remained far less ostentatious than those of many of the American houses such as Morgan Stanley with its art collections. Having outgrown the space in the Shin-Kasumigaseki Building in Tokyo, Baring Securities in Japan took over two floors of the newly built New Otani Garden Court, next door to the expensive, four-star New Otani Hotel. One of the leading attractions of this new location to ex-patriate staff was the ability to order full English breakfast from the hotel's room service that was delivered by bow-tied waiters directly to their dealing room desks. This irritated the Japanese staff to such an extent that they finally managed to have the practice banned on the grounds that the smell lingered in the office afterwards. The ex-pat breakfasters were thwarted despite vehemently arguing that the smell of bacon and eggs was infinitely more pleasant than that of *osembe*, the Japanese rice crackers which the local staff munched on throughout the day, or indeed that of the cigarette smoke which billowed around the Japanese salesmen whose ashtrays resembled hedgehogs by the close of business because they smoked only half of each cigarette then stubbed it out vertically.

In Singapore the firm's offices opened in Ocean Towers, a gleaming, glass-fronted building in Raffles Place at the heart of the nation's business district, graced with a foyer sculpture entitled *Soaring Aspirations* which Nick Leeson walked past each day. Ominously the firm had taken over the twenty-fourth floor, shunned by the locals for its unlucky number. In Hong Kong, Baring Securities became the first tenant of the newly built, highrise, mirror-and-stone Exchange Square development overlooking the harbour. In London the firm moved from Portsoken Street to a plush new Art Deco-style headquarters with miles of glinting chrome at No. 1 America Square, just down the road from Barings' head offices, which were still at No. 8 Bishopsgate where they had been since 1806, although they no longer owned the site, having sold the freehold in the 1980s. It is now owned by the German property investment company Deutsche Immobilien Fonds AG.

Baring Securities' expansion programme was remarkable for the rate of its growth, the scale of its success and the fact that it sustained this success for an extremely long period. The firm seemed to have a Midas touch. It came from Christopher Heath's original vision as to how the business was to be developed and to that extent the expansion was a self-fulfilling prophecy; the most remarkable fact was that the firm generated enough revenue from Japan to follow its expansion programme through.

Heath's aim was to diversify the company's earnings beyond Japan by moving into other emerging Asian markets. It was his philosophy that expansion would be best accomplished, and the company's profile accordingly raised, if the drive into South East Asia focused on providing the best research on local markets. Heath believed that good research was the only legitimate vehicle for sales and 'the way to build up a long term franchise. If you had really high quality research then people would have to deal with you.'

Whereas in the mid-Eighties most broking firms had only a handful of analysts dedicated to the whole of Asia, who were usually based in one centre, Hong Kong or Tokyo, Baring Securities' philosophy was to establish local teams of analysts in the capital of each of the countries that was being researched. A network of local offices was set up throughout the region headed by candidates chosen for their local and professional knowledge and supported by analysts who were hand-picked according to their individual expertise on local sectors and markets. Not only were they good, but they were well connected, visiting local companies regularly and absorbed in their environment on a daily basis. Collectively, these individuals formed excellent teams and produced detailed, high-quality regional and global research. Their ability to generate good ideas about local companies and markets put the firm squarely on the map at an early stage.

As early as 1988 the company's Japanese research was ranked first in the UK Extel Survey and the firm was voted highest-ranking foreign broker for its Japanese service in a private survey among UK institutions investing in the Far East. From 1990 to 1995 Baring Securities was ranked the best producer of overall emerging market research by international institutional investors in surveys conducted by *Asiamoney*, *Euromoney*, Extel Financial, *Global Investor*, Greenwich Associates and *Institutional Investor*. In 1994 Barings was named Best Securities Firm in Asia in *Euromoney*'s Award for Excellence because they: 'provide the most insightful and well-presented research available on the Asian market . . . offer services in equities, derivatives, options, warrants, convertibles and country funds . . . [and] have high calibre individuals who flourish in their markets.'

The blossoming network of research offices throughout Asia provided a solid foundation for Baring Securities' sales and trading activities in the region, which progressed either in the form of tactical alliances with local stockbroking firms or, where possible, in the acquisition of seats on the local exchanges.

In addition to forging the way for Baring Securities' burgeoning profitability across South East Asia, this expansion also triggered the beginnings of a dispute with Baring Brothers which took on various guises, both professional and personal, over the following years, but was never fully resolved. This conflict derived from the relationship between the business conducted by the two companies. It was clear from the success of the US investment banks, that there were natural synergies between the two businesses and both Securities and Brothers recognized that there were benefits to combining, or at least collaborating on, a wide variety of different projects. Disagreement usually arose from how such collaboration should be organized, managed or controlled.

One clear case for collaboration in the mid-Eighties was in the IPO market in Asia. An Initial Public Offering, literally the first shares offered to the public for sale by a previously unlisted company, was an excellent way for emerging Asian companies to raise money cheaply to fuel their expansion and at the same time heighten their corporate profile both locally and internationally, so that at a later date they could issue bonds or apply for bank loans. This was a market that Baring Brothers was keen to earn fees from by arranging and underwriting new IPO deals. Similarly, Baring Securities was eager to be involved so that it could gain access to a supply of this paper to meet the demand from its investor client base. Collaboration between the various departments in the two companies worked very well in terms of gaining business and Barings became unquestionably the leading IPO arranger and distributor in Asia, but irritations remained about whose efforts and status had succeeded in capturing the business.

Baring Brothers had had a presence in Asia since the days of the British Empire when banking spoils had been divided up between the Rothschilds and Barings, the Rothschilds taking Europe, while Barings flew the flag east of Suez. All the old British Far Eastern trading companies such as Jardine Matheson, Swires and Inchcape, had banked with Barings, but by the Eighties the banking business was semi-dormant, providing a marginal existence rather than an overtly profitable one. Nevertheless, Baring Brothers pointed to these in-depth historical ties, while Baring Securities countered with its pre-eminence in research and broking throughout the region which, they argued, had provided the Brothers with the profile to make them a contender. In actual fact, the one's history complemented the other's racy, entrepreneurial image very well, and vice versa, but the initial perceptions when Baring Securities was created had set a bad precedent. Given the different backgrounds of Securities and Brothers it was not surprising that rivalry between the two developed. In most instances it was perfectly healthy and enhanced the competitiveness of the whole, but it was not always viewed so internally. Andrew Baylis remembers: 'When we went to Barings it was perceived as a second division player. While it had a name of great historical repute, it wasn't a leading light in the financial world outside the United Kingdom and Baring Securities transformed its profile both in terms of the media and its international reach and reputation. It was probably rather provoking if you were in the bank, to think here was this *arriviste* organization in danger of becoming the tail that wagged the dog. It's only human nature to be sensitive to that.'

The broking arm viewed Baring Brothers as a sleepy merchant bank which had long needed someone to come along and shake it up. As profits grew at Baring Securities and its reputation and profile were enhanced, it also took the credit for raising Baring Brothers' profile and bringing it new business. The attention which Baring Securities' success attracted in the financial press undoubtedly raised the profile of the bank and breathed life back into the crusty 200-year-old institution, but Baring Brothers felt that Securities was to an extent taking all the credit for the historical business relationships which it had built up by long-term commitment to its banking clients globally. As far as they were concerned Baring Securities had, far from shaking them up, simply come along at a time when the markets were being shaken up anyway.

'There was a perception that the banking business was not that profitable, whereas the broking operation evidently was,' explains a senior Brothers executive in Hong Kong. 'There was an economic imbalance. While the brokers were making the social columns, the bankers were quite defensive about their business.'

Despite rifts between Securities and Brothers there were protracted periods of co-operation which allowed the company to present a unified face and were significant in developing business and generating substantial profitability. Business was successfully pursued despite the two sides' differences.

The benefits to be reaped from co-operation were demonstrated in Hong Kong specifically in the mid-Eighties, where, despite personal friction between the two camps, the success of collaborative efforts between the Brothers and Securities provided a role model for the rest of the company. Baring Brothers' Hong Kong corporate finance department had been dormant in the early Eighties. Its first corporate finance activity had been in 1961 when it had taken Jardine Matheson public, but after that it had done very little. Since 1984, however, under the guidance of Andrew Tuckey in London, the Brothers had been rejuvenating their corporate finance business and wanted to take advantage of the distribution channels offered to them by the securities arm. In 1986 the bank, under the leadership of Nigel Melville, gained great cachet in Hong Kong when they took the joint lead with Wardley in floating Cathay Pacific and distributing the paper through the broking side of the firm. It was the biggest IPO ever in Hong Kong and a phenomenal success. From late 1986 to October 1987 the two sides built on this accomplishment by assisting a great many Hong Kong property companies with equity issues and in 1989 they sold the Hong Kong government's remaining 10 per cent stake in Hong Kong Telecom, a $550 million transaction, to considerable acclaim.

Despite the role model of co-operation presented by the Hong Kong endeavours, relations between the bankers and brokers remained decidedly patchy in some offices in Asia as a result of their differing outlooks towards their respective businesses. Tokyo, for example, as the primary base for the Securities' profitability, saw particular friction, most notably over warrant business.

Baring Brothers hoped that Securities' position as the leading house in the Japanese equity warrant market would help to bring it greater involvement in the underwriting and issuance of these deals. However, Brothers was unable to break the stranglehold of the large Japanese firms and was relatively unsuccessful at securing consistent senior underwriting positions, despite the Securities pre-eminence in the secondary (post-issue trading) market. It never attained the position of lead manager for a dollar-warrant deal, though it did lead manage some warrant issues in more obscure currencies. Baring Securities argued that this was because the bank had never put the resources or manpower behind it and had therefore not been sufficiently proactive in soliciting deals, while the Brothers maintained that it was simply impossible for them to overcome the dominance of the Japanese houses; indeed, no foreign underwriter ever has.

During 1986 when the Japanese and Far Eastern markets were at their busiest ever, Baring Securities produced colossal profits, up by more than 100 per cent on its first year of operation. Before the October 1987 crash, the Securities were providing over two-thirds of the bank's profits. The tiny broking firm that John Baring had paid £6 million for in 1984 had, in its first two years, become by far the largest chunk of a bank established before the French Revolution.

The apparently unstaunchable stream of profits flowing in from the Japanese warrant business provided the key to meeting the bill for Baring Securities' expansion, but the problem about these earnings was that there was no guarantee of their sustainability. By the end of the Eighties, concerns over future profitability and the maintenance of the company's competitiveness overall kindled the Brothers' interest in establishing closer links with its sister company. In the early Nineties this was to grow into a desire for full integration as the Brothers increasingly felt that the creation of a whole would produce more than the sum of the two parts.

Although Securities had adopted a highly individual, if somewhat freewheeling, approach to business in its early years, it was all the more remarkable for the fact that it had also maintained its professional integrity and standing in the market as a whole. However, as the firm grew dramatically, the need for a more formal management structure, more authoritative managers and stricter financial and directional controls had become increasingly apparent. This was being addressed at the time by Christopher Heath, but he was looking for a structural solution, whereas the Brothers wanted to address it culturally. Heath hired a new Finance Director, Ian Martin, whose role eventually developed into that of Chief Operating Officer responsible for most of the functional areas of the business outside sales, research and trading. Martin set up a Business Development Group – the members of which became known as 'Martin's henchmen' – who would parachute in to fire-fight specific problems and check up on the workings of local offices in the absence of any internal audit function. The Business Development Group was Martin's means of imposing a control structure to counter-balance Heath's hands-off approach to management and the laissez-faire culture of the company.

However, these attempts neither satisfied the Brothers, nor did they satisfy those within Securities. Managers who were brought in from outside tended to be resented by old hands who didn't feel they had a worthwhile role to play or, in some cases, that their presence was even necessary. 'A lot of people in the front side didn't like it,' says Heath, 'because they thought these guys were interfering with the business. Some of them objected really strongly and said: "Who are all these guys and what are they doing? How much are they costing us? Get rid of them. We don't need them." There was quite a lot of troop resistance – perhaps the failure was in not educating people as to exactly what the objectives of the business development side were, rather than having these guys appearing from nowhere.'

The crucial difference between the two sides was Securities' persistence in maintaining its independence. 'We were insistent on rowing our own boat and keeping at arm's length from the bank, and that produced friction and some jealousy, particularly when things were going well,' says Andrew Baylis. 'We were the cheeky upstart, the cuckoo in the nest. It pleased them because of the profile and the money, but we were a stone in their shoe.'

To the Brothers, 19 October 1987 looked as if it might provide an opportunity for reconciliation and the reconstruction of their relationship with Securities. The world's stock markets crashed and the Baring Securities party looked as if it might be over. The pendulum had swung in the bank's favour. The bankers thought that by linking the two arms of the business they could offer mutual support to one another; the bank would gain improved business opportunities and the brokers more stable earnings.

The swing was to last only a week, however. The Japanese economy was still sufficiently buoyant to withstand the shock of the crash; the Japanese stock market, which by then accounted for 45 per cent of the world stock markets' value, was affected less than any other market and bounced back aggressively to hit new highs. In the week which followed 19 October, dealings in the warrant market were frenetic and Baring Securities recouped all of its losses and more. As Japan remained the core of Securities' business, Heath and his team enjoyed an extraordinarily rapid and unexpected return to profitability. In the mean time, the initial attempt by the Brothers to open up a dialogue on integration had unfortunately led to an aggressive and heated debate. When the markets crashed, the head of one of the bank's regional offices marched into that of his counterpart in Securities, jabbed a finger at him and yelled derisively, 'You're bust!' The Securities man rose from his desk, grabbed him by the collar and tie and shouted back: 'Don't you tell me we're bust. You don't know the first thing about this business.' A senior Brothers executive remembers: 'The crash could have acted as a catalyst in bringing the two businesses together, but actually it did the opposite. The old banker/broker tension was heightened and then, when the broking business recovered so dramatically, the brokers' memories were only of the bad things that had been said about them at the time of the crash.'

The markets were tougher in 1988 than in 1987 and many securities houses began to cut back, but Baring Securities continued its stellar growth, expanding its staff to 520 – an increase of 30 per cent. That year it won the first of two Queen's Awards for Export Achievement, the only securities firm to have done so. Amusingly, after the award one Japanese business magazine mistakenly credited Barings as having been newly appointed as stockbroker to the Queen, which certainly did no harm to business in Japan.

In 1988 the firm became a full member of the Australian Stock Exchange, the New York Stock Exchange and the Tokyo Stock Exchange. New offices were opened in Frankfurt, Geneva and Paris to cover European markets. In the US, teams were set up in New York and Los Angeles selling all markets covered by the company to a North American institutional client base, and by 1990 Baring Securities had opened its first Latin American office in Mexico City. Profitability dropped some 25 per cent from 1987 to 1988 as a result of expenditure on the rapid expansion programme, but it was still a remarkable achievement based so heavily on the revenues of just one product: Japanese warrants.

'Post-crash, Baring Securities continued to expand its presence around the Asian region. It was usually the first, or among the first, to establish a physical presence in each market. The potential for flow-on business for the bank was substantial,' says a bank executive. 'The markets themselves were beginning to get attention worldwide and the capital needs of the region were significant, giving rise to equity financing and privatization opportunities.' The bank's desire for integration grew even greater as the potential for profits through collaboration with Securities grew ever larger, but Heath retained his independent stance and, following the swift rebound after the crash, still had the profitability and ongoing high profile of Securities to fend off any pressure from the bank. A London-based Brothers executive recalls: 'Christopher was untouchable in 1989.'

The professional differences between Brothers and Securities by the early Nineties – which boiled down to a fundamental difference in their respective views as to how to maintain competitiveness in a changing financial industry – had become unbridgeable. This situation was aggravated not only by a wealth of smaller cultural issues, but by a growing litany of personal issues that arose not in small part due to Heath's elevated public profile.

Because the remuneration formula was based on Baring Securities' profitability, packages paid to senior Securities staff were, in some years, remarkable even by City standards. One of the biggest blows came in October 1987 when Christopher Heath, having finally been voted on to the Baring Brothers board and therefore for the first time been obliged to publicly announce his remuneration package, hit the headlines and became a media sensation as Britain's highest-paid man with reported earnings for 1986 of £2.5 million. His Kensington home was besieged by reporters. These figures were for the financial year ending 30 September, nineteen days before Black Monday. It was made clear in the press that, although this was the officially published figure, Heath's final entitlements under the profit-sharing scheme suggested ultimate earnings of more like £5 million. The wealthy board members at Baring Brothers were beginning to feel like paupers.

Heath pinpoints the beginning of the final debacle to this time. 'The jealous eye started to come into the picture when we started making a lot of money and then unfortunately I got that publicity. I think that set people thinking round at No. 8. They started to get worried when we expanded pretty rapidly and continued to be very successful, seemingly not having very many problems along the way.' However, a former senior executive of the bank denies that there was anything personal in the friction between the two camps: 'I don't think it was a problem. Most people like success and enjoy others' success as long as it is non-threatening to their own.'

Baring Brothers had been in a conciliatory mood in 1987, but by 1991 Tuckey and Baring's vision of a future integrated investment bank had taken strong root and the bank merely awaited an opportunity for their plan to be implemented. This would almost certainly mean losing Heath, and that could easily damage the franchise he had built up, which the Brothers could ill afford to do. The bank needed to find a suitable successor to Heath. The timing was crucial to any confrontation with Heath; if he was still in his ascendancy it would be impossible to successfully lobby the support of his management team. The downturn of the Japanese stock market in the early Nineties provided the Brothers with the opportunity, and a young corporate finance star returning from a Hong Kong posting provided them with the candidate.

5 | The Parmiter's Boy

'Nick is no Jack-the-lad. He was a normal young lad who
decided he was going to do well in life.'
ALEC SIMS, FATHER-IN-LAW

While Christopher Heath was building up his Asian empire, the
young school-leaver Nick Leeson had been taking the first steps
towards carving out a financial career for himself in the City of
London. Their paths were to cross in 1989 when Heath was at the
height of his power and Leeson, with two jobs already under his
belt, had just joined Baring Securities, having recognized the opportunities for advancement that such a firm could offer an ambitious
back office clerk like himself.

The twenty-eight-year-old trader who brought down the City's
oldest bank, achieving worldwide notoriety in the process, came
from humble roots in Watford, Hertfordshire. Nicholas William
Leeson was born on 25 February 1967 to Anne and William Leeson, and spent the first years of his life in a small flat in Orbital
Crescent, North Watford. As the family grew larger, they moved
to a modest three-bedroom, end-of-terrace council house in Haines
Way, Garston, an estate on the northern edge of Watford. Only
twenty miles separated the back garden of the house where Leeson
grew up from the Barings' boardroom in the City.

Leeson's father William, known by his friends as Harry, was a
self-employed plasterer, travelling around the country six or seven
days a week to earn a living. His mother Anne was a nurse at the
Leavesden Mental Hospital until she died from cancer in 1987.
After the death of his mother, Nick, then aged twenty, helped his
father to raise his younger siblings: Richard, now twenty-six, and
two younger sisters, Vicky and Sarah. His father was popular in
the local community and regarded as a man who prided himself on

looking after and supporting his children. Despite working long hours, he found time to enjoy a drink with friends at weekends at his local pub, The Hare, and was often seen around the neighbourhood in plaster-splattered overalls.

Nick attended Kingsway Junior School, Garston, before moving in 1978 to another state school, Parmiter's, where his siblings were also educated. Parmiter's is a grant-maintained comprehensive, an offspring of the now defunct Parmiter's Grammar school in Bethnal Green, East London, established in 1720 with the motto '*Nemo Sibi Nascitur*: No man is born unto himself'. At the age of fifteen he met the Queen, whose bank he was to bring down, when she officially opened the school's new buildings.

The picture later to be painted by colleagues at Barings in Singapore of an arrogant man, who, in displays of high spirits, had a tendency to drop his trousers, is not one recognized by friends and family at home in England. Schoolfriends remember Leeson as bright but ordinary. 'He didn't stand out. He was just a normal bloke who liked all the ordinary things like football,' says an old classmate. He particularly enjoyed football, becoming striker for the school's first team and also played for the local Abbots Langley Football Club. He was to keep up the game later in life, captaining the Old Parmiterian team for two years after he left school and later playing for Barings' company sides in both London and Singapore.

In the wake of the Barings' crash, staff at his school were stunned by the new-found infamy of the pupil they had always regarded as fundamentally steady. According to Brian Coulshed, the headmaster, there was nothing in Leeson's school career to suggest an erratic personality or a propensity to gamble. 'He was a thoroughly dependable member of the school. Out of perhaps 120 pupils in his year he was one of 30 prefects selected by staff. He was an asset to the school.'

Neighbours and relatives describe him as being 'fantastic, keen and diligent', as well as supportive of his younger siblings and father after the death of his mother. His father-in-law, printer Alec Sims, endorsed this view after the bank's crash. 'Nick is no Jack-the-lad. He was a normal young lad who decided he was going to do well in life. He was well educated and is well spoken and is not the sort who normally becomes a dealer. Generally they are loud, brash and flash, but Nick was none of these things. He is a genuinely nice guy and I'm proud to call him a son-in-law.'

Nick took his O-levels in June 1983, gaining an A for maths, three Bs and two Cs. However, his academic work petered away in the sixth form. He failed his maths A-level completely, a fact which was to stun the British public later, but attained a C in English literature and a D in history. Brian Coulshed thinks 'he was a good mathematician. It may be that he did not work as hard in the sixth form as he did in his O levels.'

Nick was not, according to his former teachers, university material, so he opted for a career path which many in his school had taken before him: finance. A steady stream of Parmiterians had made the short journey from their East London school to the City's financial institutions and Parmiter's had tried to retain these links after its relocation, with some success: one of its old boys is a former Governor of the Bank of Canada.

In the summer of 1985, Leeson applied to half a dozen banks and was accepted by Coutts & Co., another of the Queen's banks, with a reputation for excellent service and exclusivity, catering for the highest echelons of society. Leeson joined the firm's Lombard Street Branch where he worked in the general banking division. He stayed at Coutts for two years performing back office clerical work, before moving to US bankers Morgan Stanley in June 1987. His position at Morgan's – as a futures and options settlements clerk – was also relatively lowly, but one where a motivated child of the Eighties could learn some of the mysteries of merchant banking. Staff at Morgan Stanley remember him as being unremarkable. He was 'quiet and unpretentious', says a former colleague of Leeson's. Another woman I spoke to who had worked in the same department with him for over a year was astonished when she heard of his exploits as she could not even remember him.

Baring Securities was at the height of its research-driven probe into South East Asia at this time. The foundation laid by the firm's network of research offices had paved the way for its sales and trading activities in the emerging markets, the success of which meant that a vastly increased volume of trades were being booked through the company. Most of the firm's expansion to date had been in what is called the front office, which encompasses research teams, sales staff and traders, as well as the new management that Heath was bringing in to oversee the whole operation. As a consequence, the back office, the department which settles trades and accounts for the company, had fallen behind.

Throughout the Eighties, most British broking firms, including Baring Securities, had very primitive systems for dealing with the clearance of trades. Prior to the introduction in the early Nineties of central clearance corporations – which accept the stock from one counterparty and arrange payment to the other and whose risk is underwritten by a group of banks – trades were settled directly between the parties involved. One party would arrange physical delivery of the stock and the other would send a cheque back to cover the cost. Sizeable trades could engender enormous financial risks; one party might have given away its stock, only to discover that the cheque from the other had failed to clear.

The 1987 crash, when huge volumes of trades were put through brokerage firms, had exposed the deficiencies of their back offices. Indeed, this was one of the major causes of Baring Brothers' concern about the way the Securities operation was being run. Baring Securities found itself in crisis at that time and was forced to hire teams of external auditors to help settle their trades. In the wake of the crash, Heath realized that a greater emphasis needed to be placed on boosting the capabilities of the back office and upgrading the systems. Nick Leeson and Lisa Sims, his future wife, were both hired by Baring Securities as stockbrokers' clerks as part of Heath's move to address this problem.

In effect, settlements staff look after 80 per cent of the work associated with completing any single trade once it has been made. As soon as the front office has concluded a transaction, the back office takes over the details of putting the trade into the system, organizing the deliverer and buyer instructions, making certain the currencies and amounts match – often arranging the foreign exchange themselves – then sending the instructions to the global custodian and ensuring that the trade settles on the appointed day so that neither party loses money. In addition to knowing how the individual markets work, they also have to learn the intricate technicalities of withholding tax and capital gains tax that may affect certain trades or clients, thus relieving the front office of a great deal of mundane work.

Good stockbroking clerks also look for angles which will benefit the front office by saving money or speeding up settlements. There is a marked contrast between a stockbrokers clerk and a bankers clerk. 'A bankers clerk is an A–Z sharp cookie. He's well versed and well qualified, but he does his job from nine to five with no questions asked and then he goes home. The stockbrokers clerk always asks why he's there; he's always saving time, cutting corners for the benefit of the company, whereas the bankers clerk wouldn't even see the corners to cut,' a long-serving back office employee explained to me.

Despite the obvious necessity for efficient back office staff, they remain second-class citizens in the brokerage world. The same member of Barings' settlements department complained to me over a beef roll and a pint in a City pub: 'We're not on the map. We're purely back office. The traders think that we're just the chaps who put the trades into the system and, when the trade is finished, close it down. They think that's our sole function.' Baring Securities back office staff were highly motivated and well rewarded in industry terms, but the industry's general lack of appreciation for this work leads to frustration and an ambition, particularly on the part of younger employees, to join the front office where both the recognition and financial benefits are far greater.

Nick Leeson joined the settlements department of Baring Securities in July 1989 on a salary of about £12,000, working initially on the treasury functions of the company. According to a former colleague, he was good at his job: 'If you weren't good, you were shown the back door. There was no room for people to hide in corners at Barings.' However, he was not renowned for being overtly sociable. 'I got to know him in the way one does, bumping into him in the corridor or the loo,' says a staff member who worked with him then. 'He didn't mix very much and I don't think he does now. He was quiet and I find it hard to believe that he's the kind of chap who drops his strides in public, but then I suppose when you're in a foreign country . . .'

Lisa Sims, a pretty twenty-one-year-old who lived at home with her parents and enjoyed exercise and aerobics in her spare time, was hired in March 1990.

Born in South London in 1969 to Alec and Patsy, she moved to a quiet, modern cul-de-sac in the small village of West Kingsdown, Kent, when she was four, where she and her younger sister Nadine and brother Al were brought up. She attended the local Swanley Comprehensive, where she was a popular, extrovert pupil. She was considered lucky by her friends, many of whom became secretaries and office workers, when she gained her A-levels in accountancy and economics and embarked on a career in the city.

A few days after leaving school, she began work as a settlements clerk at Nikko Securities, a Japanese broking firm. It was 1986 and boom time in the City, and she was poached a year or so later by Swiss Bank. She remained with Swiss Bank Corporation until 1990, when the company began laying off a number of its employees. Keen to move on before her own number was called, she went for an interview at Barings.

Barings had recently identified the need for a new liaison team to take the pressure off salesmen who, despite the fact that the firm had by then switched the settlement of its South East Asian trades from London to the Asian offices, were still being pestered by clients with settlement problems. Lisa was hired to make up a team of four which would liaise between the firm's clients and its South East Asian offices except Japan, thus relieving the sales desk of the burden. 'She was tremendous with the clients. She had a bubbly, effervescent approach to all the people she met,' recalls a staff member who worked on her team. 'She was a lovely girl. The photos don't do her credit. She was very pretty.'

According to her friends and colleagues Lisa was very natural. 'Your first impression was that this was a girl you could sit down and talk to for ages and get honest answers,' recalls a male contemporary of Lisa's. 'She would give her opinions on anything, she always told you exactly what she thought. She was attractive but she was the kind of person who became more attractive when you got to know her personality. The kind of girl you could fall in love with.'

Baring Securities was a vibrant, young people's company and a combination of long working days and after-hours drinks with colleagues in the evening spawned many office romances and a high proportion of marriages to follow. The London settlements department had a tremendous sense of camaraderie and back office employees often remained with the firm, not for the money, but because they enjoyed working with each other. Lisa and Nick often went out drinking and dancing with their colleagues, in the course of which they got to know one another better.

In 1990 Barings, like several other foreign firms, developed problems in Indonesia. The number of transactions on the local exchange by Far Eastern brokers had risen dramatically and Barings was the biggest foreign broker in the market. Locally, custodian banks and processors couldn't cope with the volumes of paper work involved and Baring Securities' own back office staff, who were all locals, were equally overwhelmed by the number of trades which needed to be settled. The company and its clients were in danger of losing money. Baring Securities Jakarta needed a team of experienced, European settlements staff who were familiar with the system to sort out the internal problems and liaise with foreign clients directly.

By that time Nick Leeson had become one of 'Martin's Henchmen' – a member of the Business Development Group set up by Ian Martin to firefight just this sort of problem. Leeson was chosen to head up a team of four men to deal with the situation. They were posted first to Hong Kong, which ran the Indonesian operation, to analyse the problems at that end, and then to Jakarta. Lisa was later sent out to join them. Baring Securities was the first foreign broker to spot the problem and resolve it, and their quick resolution of the situation won them an invitation to sort out Hong Kong Bank's settlements department. Consequently, Baring Securities ended up actually making money from the Indonesian problem while some other foreign brokerage houses lost substantial sums.

During the period when her daughter was away, Lisa's mother, Patsy, who worked in an office in London, faxed messages to Baring Securities' London office, which in turn faxed them on to Lisa in Jakarta. 'Lisa was a very family-oriented person. She was always talking about her Mum and Dad and her uncle and brother. They were very genuine people,' says a former colleague. Both Nick and Lisa loved Jakarta and made many good friends there. They sat next to each other at work and spent all their time together, going out in a group with people from the office at weekends, as was the tradition in Barings' Asian offices. During their time abroad, isolated from the support of their old friends and family, they also came to appreciate one another's company more. Lisa was attracted by Nick's quiet aura of control: 'When I first met him, I just assumed he was the one in charge. It wasn't like: "Wow, this is the man I'm going to marry", but I liked him. He was always kind and we would chat.'

When the Jakarta job was completed, the ex-pats were recalled to London. It was then that the cat was let out of the bag: Nick and Lisa, whose relationship had blossomed in foreign climes, were engaged. Reluctant to continue working in the same department as her fiancé, Lisa moved on to the South East Asian desk in the front office to work as an assistant to the dealers.

Colleagues recall how excited Lisa and Nick were about the wedding. 'Excited is an understatement,' said a male contemporary of Lisa's who heard all about the plans during the course of each working day. 'She couldn't stop talking about it.' The couple tied the knot in March of 1992, at St Edmund the King church just down the road from Lisa's parents house in West Kingsdown. The wedding was followed by a reception at the Brand's Hatch Thistle Hotel. A friend remembers it as 'a posh occasion. It was a father giving the daughter he loved dearly the best he could.' The wedding cost some £20,000. The newlyweds went on honeymoon on the Orient Express to Venice.

Since his return from Jakarta, Leeson had continued to work on special projects for the Business Development Group. In September and October of 1991, Leeson took charge of a special investigation by Baring Securities into a case of apparent fraud in the derivatives area between a Barings' employee and a client. The client had been using his own clients' investment funds illicitly, by actively trading them on a proprietary basis; Barings had been led to believe that their client *was* a proprietary trader. When the client began to lose substantial sums, a Barings' employee allegedly colluded with him to suppress a report that showed the late margin calls. Leeson did an excellent job of investigating the problem and getting the situation back on track. The question which inevitably arises is whether Leeson got any ideas from this experience. As the settlements supervisor had been dismissed along with the offending employee following the fraud case, Leeson then took charge of the settlement of Japanese futures and options trades – experience which was to prove invaluable to him later.

As a reward for his successes in Jakarta and in London, in April 1992, just a month after the wedding, Nick's application to be posted to Singapore was granted. An increasing amount of Baring Securities' burgeoning futures and options business in Tokyo was heading towards Singapore in 1992 as a result both of the clients' desire to trade on the exchange there and because commission charges on SIMEX were lower than those on the Japanese exchanges. When Nick heard that the firm was setting up a new futures operation in Singapore, he requested to be sent out to organize the settlements and accounting departments and head up the SIMEX floor operation. 'He was likeable, reliable and extremely competent. Having solved the equity problems in Jakarta, it was thought he could do it alone,' explains a member of the futures and options broking team.

To all concerned, the honest, hardworking Leeson was the ideal candidate for the task. There was, however, a question mark over his integrity, but one which went unremarked by his firm.

In February 1992, before he took up the Singapore posting, Leeson had applied to the Securities and Futures Authority for a City of London trading licence. Under the terms of the Financial Services Act, securities and futures companies must be authorized by the SFA to do investment business and all individuals employed

by those firms in positions of authority – directors, certain cate-
gories of managers and all those trading or involved in managing
clients' portfolios – are also required to be licensed by the SFA.

Baring Securities submitted Leeson's SFA application, in which
his response to the question of whether he had any county court
judgments outstanding against him was 'No'. The SFA does a routine financial check into all applicants and discovered that Leeson
did have one outstanding judgment. In May 1992 Watford County
Court had made a judgment of £2,426 against him on behalf of
National Westminster Bank.

Christopher Sharples, the SFA Chairman, says: 'We didn't reject
his application. We simply pointed out that he had been untruthful
in terms of the application form – honesty is a very important part
of licensing in the financial services industry – and referred it back
to Barings for them to decide what to do. They just withdrew it
without another word and that was the end of it. Leeson was then
in Singapore very shortly after that.' The SFA might not have
automatically banned Leeson from trading if he had declared the
county court judgment, but he would have been asked for an explanation and told to settle the debt before he started. 'If he'd admitted
to it, given some justification and if he'd repaid his debts and cleared
the county court judgment, the likelihood is that, subject to probably a probationary period when he'd be told to be under special
supervision by someone else at Barings, he'd have been given a
licence,' says Sharples.

In fact, Leeson appears to have run up more than this one debt
of £2,426 in the two years before he went to Singapore. According
to Chris Brogan, Managing Director of the International Commercial Agency Limited, a total of £10,047 in county court judgments
had been registered against Leeson during this period, most of
which were paid off. It is perhaps worth noting that this is not
unusual among young people starting out in the City. While their
salaries are high relative to those of employees in other sectors,
they find themselves surrounded by colleagues who earn substantially larger sums of money and who often spend it freely. Such an
environment encourages them to spend beyond their means in an
attempt to keep up with their peers, often in the expectation that

Above right: 'Yes, I'm the man you want': Nick and Lisa Leeson were detained by German police at Frankfurt airport on 2 March 1995 as they stepped off a plane from Brunei, ending a six-day international manhunt.

Inset: Nick Leeson in 1983 at Parmiter's School, motto: 'No man is born unto himself'. The new-found notoriety of Leeson, a prefect, shocked his former teachers who had always considered him 'fundamentally steady'.

Right: Behind bars: Nick Leeson in Preungeshelm Prison in the Frankfurt suburb of Höchst, Germany, where he was held pending extradition to Singapore.

Traders at the Singapore International Monetary Exchange in open outcry in the pit where Leeson made his fatal derivatives trades.

Pit Bull: Nick Leeson at work on the SIMEX trading floor where he was known as '. . . the most confident trader around town', 'a king with a 'Midas touch'.

Above: Boat Quay by night with Singapore's smart
business district in the background.

Inset: Favourite bar, favourite tipple.

Below: Inside Harry's Quayside, where Leeson drank
nightly with his colleagues and listened to jazz bands.

Lisa in happier times.

Lisa dresses up for showtime with the girls.

Rear view of the
Leesons' Angullia View
apartment block.

Above: 'I want you all on the phones!' Christopher Heath in the Baring Securities (Japan) office on the firm's first day of trading on the Tokyo Stock Exchange in June, 1988.

Right: Heath gives the thumbs up as another order floods in.

Ron Baker, head of the fated
Financial Products Group.

Impending bombshell:
Peter Norris, Chief Executive Officer
of Barings Investment Bank.

James Bax, Regional Manager
for South Asia: 'Singapore is
full of landmines, and
I know where they are.'

Caught on a train: Peter Baring, Barings' Chairman, had always shunned the press. Here he reads that the bank he has served all his life has been bought by Dutch financial giant ING.

Andrew Tuckey, Barings' Deputy Chairman, was hoping to lead the firm into its future as an integrated investment bank.

Right: A member of the Financial Products Group makes light of the Barings saga at the Hong Kong Rugby Sevens, March 1995.

Below: 'Don't throw my Nick to the wolves': a tearful Lisa Leeson reads out a hand-written letter from her husband at a press conference in London on 12 July 1995, in which he begged to be spared a 'show trial' in Singapore in a desperate bid to be extradited to the UK.

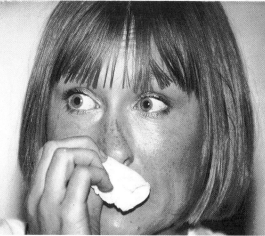

Below: The other side of the story: a Barings' employee hangs his head in despair during the week of uncertainty following the collapse.

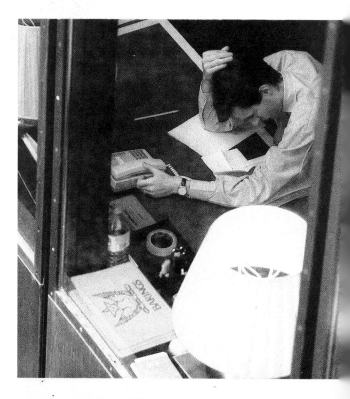

On 6 March 1995 ING bought substantially all the businesses, assets and liabilities of the Baring Group as a going concern for £1. The real cost of the acquisition was in the ensuing recapitalization; a cash injection of almost £700 million.

future salary increases or bonus payments will make up the shortfall.

In addition to this personal warning signal, a professional one had also been sounded, but this too had gone unheeded by the executives at Baring Securities in London.

Nick Leeson was sent out to Singapore by Ian Martin, by then the Chief Operating Officer of Baring Securities, to head the SIMEX operation. The Singapore office was headed by James Bax, who, during his preliminary interviews with Baring Securities, had made a feature of his knowledge that: 'Singapore is full of landmines and I know where they are', a phrase which no doubt haunts him retrospectively. But on 25 March 1992, a month before Leeson's arrival in Singapore, Bax sent a fax to Andrew Fraser, then Head of South East Asian Broking and Trading at Barings in London, in which he expressed concern over Leeson's role.

'My concern is that we are once again in danger of setting up a structure that will subsequently prove disastrous and with which we will succeed in losing either a lot of money or client goodwill or probably both,' he wrote. 'In my view it is critical that we should keep clear reporting lines, and if this office is involved in SIMEX, then Nick should report to Simon [Jones] and then be ultimately responsible for the operations side.' This fax was intended to raise objections both to Leeson being sent out as 'head of our SIMEX operations' and to the fact that he had been told to report directly to London, whereas Bax wished to retain local control over the Singapore operations by having Leeson report to Simon Jones, the Singapore-based Operations Manager for South Asia. It was indicative of the tension at that time between local managers [Bax in this case] and group financial control in London. Bax concluded by warning that unless Leeson's role was limited, his own position as a senior manager was 'inappropriate and needs review'. What the fax revealed about the conflicting responsibilities in the broad role which had been laid out for Leeson is retrospectively far more ominous than it was at the time. Nevertheless, Bax's complaints should have set alarm bells ringing in London.

When Nick and his new wife Lisa arrived at Singapore's smart Changi airport in April 1992, it must have seemed as if life was about to take a turn for the better. Both had stuck their heads down at work and were about to be justly rewarded. Nick was twenty-five, Lisa twenty-three; they had left behind them a boring life in Britain and humdrum jobs in a City back office. The small flat they had bought in south-east London was about to be replaced by a spacious apartment in a prime residential district, paid for by the company. Nick's salary had doubled and all the benefits of ex-patriate living awaited them. Although Nick had been posted to a back office job not unlike the one he had had in London, he was on a promise of something better.

6 | The Turbulence

'The company had become a nest of vipers'
FORMER DIRECTOR, BARING SECURITIES

About the same time that the newly-married Leesons touched down at Changi airport in the spring of 1992, Peter Norris, returning from a five-year posting in Hong Kong, landed at Heathrow. At that stage Nick Leeson, along with most in Baring Securities, was unaware that within the year he would have a new boss.

Heath and his successor, Norris, embody the differences in both culture and long-term strategic objectives that began to emerge between Securities and Brothers in the early Nineties. The event which was to bring them to a head-on clash, culminating in a takeover of Securities management, took place, not surprisingly, in Japan, the hub and cash cow of Baring Securities. This seminal event was the most dramatic collapse in the Tokyo stock market since World War II.

In 1989, Japan was still in a euphoric dreamland of economic prosperity where stock prices had gained 29 per cent year-on-year; on the year's final trading day, the Nikkei Average popped the champagne corks when it scaled a new all-time high of 38,915.87, a record yearly gain of almost 9,000 points. Throughout 1989, however, there had been a clear threat that the Japanese bubble of overheated stock and property markets might burst at any moment and, after the festive cheer of New Year, the Tokyo market opened for business in 1990 with a decided hangover. On February 26 it saw its biggest drop since Black Monday in 1987, an indication of what lay ahead; by 1 October it had plummeted 48 per cent to a 1990 low of 20,221.86, the market's steepest crash in the post-war era, except for a brief period of market instability following the end of World War II.

By the end of 1990 the outlook for foreign brokerage firms in Japan looked grim. Income from equity broking had declined enormously because trading volume in the market had nose-dived and the average share price was at a low level, thus hitting brokerage commissions, which are calculated by taking a percentage of the share price and multiplying it by the number of shares transacted. Moreover, the Japanese Ministry of Finance had imposed a reduction in commission rates in an attempt to draw investors back to the market. There was to be no improvement in 1991 as the Japanese market saw another year of correction following the Eighties boom.

For Baring Securities, which had made a significant proportion of its profits from dealing in equity warrants during the bull market, there was an additional problem. In the five years from 1986 to 1990, backed by the buoyant stock market, Japanese corporations had issued warrant bonds worth over $150 billion, but the market's sharp decline brought a swift halt to the rush of new issues. The plunge of the Tokyo equity and bond markets and the weakness of the yen dealt a severe blow to Japanese companies which had been used to uninterrupted growth and seemingly limitless cheap financing. The credit squeeze closed down many avenues of borrowing, especially for small- and medium-sized companies, and even firms which had become cautious about refinancing given the downturn in the economy and the poor outlook for growth prospects were forced to push their relationship banks to underwrite deals despite the bad reception in the market. From March 1990 to July of the same year, the Big Four Japanese brokerage houses put a self-imposed moratorium on the new issue market. Even when the market re-opened, the flow of new warrant bond issues was very restricted and, as old warrant issues expired, the market began to die away.

The warrant market's decline was accelerated by a crisis in investor confidence in 1990 as the Nikkei's fall meant that for the first time these warrants, that were options to buy stock over a limited period of time, were reaching their maturities when the stock price was lower than the level at which the investor had an option to buy, thus for the first time in the warrant market's history, a large proportion of these warrants were expiring worthless.

By the end of 1990, foreign brokerage houses in Tokyo were forced to reconsider their positions in Japan and come up with clear strategies to deal with the downturn in markets. Soaring overheads, shrinking turnover, slumping share prices and lower commissions had all taken their toll on many of the firms which had set up in Japan during the heady bull market of the Eighties. Even the large US firms such as Salomons and Morgan Stanley began to tighten their belts by rationalizing their businesses and reducing overheads and staff, particularly high-cost expatriates. Smaller firms toyed with the idea of pulling out of Japan altogether, even with the knowledge that the authorities would make it difficult for them to regain a licence and re-enter the market in later years.

Despite the collapse of the equity and warrant markets in Japan which had been the prime sources of revenue for Baring Securities and had made a substantial contribution to the group as a whole, Barings plc managed to post better profits than many of its rivals in 1990. Other much larger UK houses such as County NatWest, Kleinwort Benson and Barclays de Zoete Wedd posted significantly lower profits than the previous year (even, in some cases, declaring losses), while Barings profits topped £40 million; this was £25 million lower than in 1989, but still a healthy return on capital employed.

Although Baring Securities was faring better than many of its competitors, there were clear warning signals to scale back operations. The sudden demise of the Japanese warrant market and the consequent staunching of one of Baring Securities' main sources of revenues exacerbated Baring Brothers' concerns about the sustainability of profits in the broking arm. Now more than ever, it was vital that the company had a clear strategy for dealing with the downturn in markets.

Heath had in fact hedged against a fall in the Japanese market. In October 1989, at Andrew Baylis's suggestion, Baring Securities had taken out a put option on the market; while this had lost money as the index continued to roar up to the 39,000 level, it paid dividends when the market dropped off rapidly in 1990, earning the company some £20 million.

To the Brothers, however, this seemed inadequate insurance

against the future. Heath was a builder and salesman; he had a clear-cut vision of the broking empire he wanted to create, but the bank believed that he had no definite idea of how he was going to pay for it in a worsening business environment. 'He insisted on building the infrastructure into what turned out to be a grinding bear market,' says a former Baring Securities branch manager. 'He hired anyone who came along with the right curriculum vitae, whatever the price. It was a classic strategic error.'

An example cited in support of this view was that of the proprietary trader hired from Salomons on a colossal package with guaranteed bonus, whose remit was to use the company's capital to take bets on the market's direction. 'It was ludicrous,' says a top Brothers executive. 'It may be viable to have ten people like him because at least 5.1 of them will be doing sensible things at any one time, but to hire one person to do it and bet the store on his getting it right even 50 per cent of the time is ridiculous.' That comment is apparently sound in sentiment, though there is no reason why ten people should get it right more often than one. A more significant point is the fact that Baring Securities did not have sufficient capital to let him trade with. The trader's first big deal was reportedly a forex forward: he went long on sterling against the Deutsch mark the week before Black Wednesday.

In financially difficult times when markets were collapsing and costs rising apparently unchecked, Heath's costly expansionist policy was seen, even by most in Baring Securities, as cavalier. Rumour even had it that an office in Latin America had been set up without a clear budget, instead $100,000 had supposedly been paid into the branch manager's personal account with instructions to call when he ran out of money. Heath dismisses such talk as rubbish. However, even his admirers began to express their unease about his lack of caution, pointing to the massive overheads already incurred by the company's expansion to date and the spiralling costs as more new offices opened and existing business faltered, most notably in the now enormous Japanese operation with in excess of three hundred staff spread across three offices, while revenues continued to plummet.

With hindsight, Heath agrees that some criticism is valid on this point. 'Having the put option perhaps lulled one into a false sense of security in that we felt we had protection against the Japanese market overall. The big mistake was in not standing back from it and saying, "Right, we've got to cut back here because this place is not going to come back." Historically, when faced with a crisis, Japan had always solved its problems. We thought that although we might be in for a tough ride on a twelve- to eighteen-month view, Japan would bounce back. However, we weren't alone in that view. Japan wrong-footed a lot of people. The problem was far more serious than anyone gave it credit for. We felt it was prudent to take out the put option on the market but we failed to back it up by reducing our overheads.'

The bank's anxieties were not just about existing costs, however, but about Heath's continued policy of expansion with no clear revenue projection that would help to offset these overheads and raise profitability. 'He was like a driver with the car in third gear and his foot flat on the floor ignoring the fact that there was a bend coming up,' says a banking executive. 'Substantial sums of money were being invested in activities which, even if they did have a prospect of return – which was unlikely in some of them – it was a pretty long-term return.'

Heath counters that *his* was the correct strategy: 'You've got to invest in this business. You've got to cast your bread upon the waters to make money. In some people's view we cast our bread too rapidly. The fruition of that expansion programme wasn't going to come about for eighteen months or so. After March 1993, South East Asia and Latin America became strong contributors, while Japan was going inexorably down. In the very short term it was wrong, but in terms of building the business it was absolutely the right strategy and I would still do the same again. I wouldn't waver from it, because if you sit still other people spot the opportunities. If we hadn't positioned ourselves early, Baring Securities wouldn't be the force it is today in emerging markets.'

The mounting concerns about Heath's leadership were, however, not simply about what was perceived to be the wrong strategy, but about his personal attitude to business. A former Baring Securities' director, who left because he saw the direction events were taking, says Heath had 'lost the plot. The success of the Eighties had gone to his head. He was interested only in his Bentleys and his race horses. He hadn't a clue what was going on. I told him in 1989 that the Nikkei had topped-out, that it would never see the same index level again this century, but he wouldn't believe it. He just didn't see it. The sophistication of the business had overtaken him.' Heath had been a brilliant Eighties broker: great with clients and a terrific leader in a bull market. However, under his leadership, Baring Securities had never known anything but continual growth. The bank believed that a more professional, strategic approach was necessary to deal with the bear market; its executives wanted to see a new man at the helm. Within Baring Securities too there was a growing feeling of alarm.

The company had grown to a size where a clearer managerial hierarchy was required and greater responsibility taken to establish formal strategy as well as stricter control over expenses, better reporting of revenues and an improved general understanding of the company's overall financial status. Heath had taken most of the strategic and management decisions himself. Many of the senior managers had worked their way up from the sales or trading desks and had little experience of broader corporate management, especially with respect to establishing and implementing long-term strategy and maintaining stringent financial controls.

Heath was aware of the necessity to transfer control to management and develop a team of more professional managers. He attempted to achieve this by involving senior managers outside the group of five at the top of the company; Regional Managers such as James Bax in Singapore and Willie Phillips in Hong Kong were asked to take a more active part in quarterly board meetings, for example. Despite this initiative, the majority of senior managers still had little management control and a poor understanding of the firm's financial status.

Since the end of 1987 Ian Martin as Finance Director had been responsible for putting the accounts in order and supplying detailed cost and revenue figures to the directors and managers. Before that there had been virtually no viable financial information in Baring Securities. However, although Martin was one of the few people who *did* understand Baring Securities' financial status, his *modus operandi* did not prove to be particularly conducive to attaining a clearer and broader dissemination of accurate financial information. A typically unsympathetic description comes from a former director who sat alongside him at board meetings: 'He was secretive by nature. He worked on the basis that knowledge was power and he wasn't going to give it away.'

In fact Martin was merely operating according to the management policy established by Heath. Daily profit and loss figures on the trading and sales books, weekly figures and monthly management accounts with risk positions were prepared by Martin. However, it was Heath's belief that managers should only be allowed to see the figures which related to their own business areas and that walls should be erected accordingly. Bax in Singapore, for instance, should not be allowed to see Hong Kong's profit figures on the basis that he should be focusing on Singapore, rather than worrying about what was happening on someone else's patch.

In addition to the new hires there was an explosion of new directors in the early Nineties, many promoted either to massage their egos or in lieu of bonuses that couldn't be paid due to the poor market conditions. By 1992 there were over fifty directors throughout Barings who sat on the Baring Securities' London board, which was a statutory board endowing the directors with fiduciary responsibilities (a commitment few had been properly advised about by the company). Although the board met quarterly, it was too unwieldy to be viewed as an efficient decision-making body. To a staggering degree, management in the fullest macro and micro sense, still fell to Heath and, to a lesser extent, the other four members of the firm's Management Committee: Baylis, Martin, Kelly and Fraser, with Roy Johnson as the company secretary, a far smaller group than actually sat in board meetings. As such, the most useful purpose board meetings could have served was as a means of efficiently distributing information about the company's strategy and state of health, but the tight control of financial information, combined with the decided lack of interest in the information that was available on the part of many of the directors, prevented this.

A former director cites the example of a 1992 London board meeting which exemplifies this situation:

> Martin began reeling off a stream of figures, revenues, staff costs and so on, but without indicating the basis of their calculation. He was in full flight when I interrupted and said, 'What's the bottom line? Are we making or losing money?' 'I don't think this is the appropriate forum for that,' Martin replied. When I pointed out that we had fiduciary responsibility for the firm's financial status by law, pandemonium broke out.

Martin has a slightly different recollection of the occasion, but the very fact that so many of the directors in the room that day remember the scene so vividly is indicative of quite how sensitive the situation had become. In defence of his position, Martin explains, 'Legally the directors probably had a right to see much more than they did, the question is how much. It was a management issue, a cultural issue. I never said directly "You can't see it." I used to say, "Why don't you go and get it from Christopher?" or "We haven't got it here." It was all designed to try and avoid them getting access other than on a "need to know basis". If they needed to know, you told them.'

Heath admits that he was anxious to keep a short rein on the amount of sensitive information widely available. 'The system wasn't as open as it might have been; the dissemination of information was as tightly controlled as it was in the bank. I've often been shocked by people I've interviewed from other organizations at the amount of confidential information that was passed down to reasonably junior levels. There had always been a bit of a mystique about how and why Baring Securities made its money and, as we weren't a public company, we didn't see why everyone in the market place should know. The people operating on the desks knew where we stood on a weekly basis and we had quarterly board meetings where all the figures were available, but there wasn't a lot of material of a fairly sensitive nature winging about.'

He is certainly correct in saying that many in the company,

directors included, were more concerned about being at the front line of the business, generating revenues, rather than spending their time poring over balance sheets and sitting in meetings. 'Some people were just not interested, to be honest,' he explains. 'Even though they were directors of the company, they were more anxious to get on with their sales and their research, in generating profits and getting a nice bonus as a result. They weren't particularly interested in what happened behind the scenes. Getting people to turn up to board meetings was a real *effort*.'

Despite this general lack of interest in financial information, Heath's policy of restricted access became particularly problematical when the firm's profitability fell and bonuses were impacted accordingly. At that point people became extremely defensive because they felt that while they had been working tremendously hard, their bonus had been cut due to losses incurred elsewhere; they wanted to know where, how, and by whom. Martin was forced into a situation whereby every time he stepped off a plane he was met with the demand: 'I want to see the information'.

The main ongoing bone of contention between Brothers and Securities was the former's desire for integration, but there were two other points of conflict which inflamed the situation, namely capital requirements and proprietary trading. Ian Martin had maintained a very fine juggling act with the balance sheet, managing to leverage Baring Securities' business to an extraordinary degree off what was an extremely limited capital base. He was keenly aware of the need to increase the capital base, partly in order to meet the capital adequacy requirements of the SFA whose ratios were subject to regulatory changes that would bring them in line with new EC proposals.

Heath took Martin's arguments to the Brothers and throughout 1991 lobbied for a more secure capital base for Securities. His demands for a cheque were fuelled in large part by his desire to continue his expansionist policy. 'The securities business is like riding a bicycle,' says Heath. 'You've got to keep pedalling or you'll fall off. I once said this to Peter [Baring], who had his arm in a sling at the time. He said, "Don't talk to me about bicycles, I've just fallen off one."'

Heath's demands were largely stymied by the fact that the bank was not prepared to entertain the idea of allowing him room to leverage Securities' business further. Despite a continuous volley of presentations and letters between Tuckey and Baring on one side, and Heath, Baylis and Martin on the other throughout 1991, the dispute over additional capital for Securities remained unresolved.

In the midst of the continuing debate, in 1991 the bank acquired a 40 per cent equity interest in Dillon, Read & Co. Inc., a leading US investment bank based in New York. The move was designed to build on the Brothers' improving fortunes in UK corporate finance and to give them a strong foothold in the highly lucrative US market where they had been singularly unsuccessful in establishing a presence on their own. For converse reasons, the proposition was equally attractive to Dillon Read. The purchase obviously created a further obstacle to Heath's campaign for additional capital as it swallowed up an estimated £70 million of Baring plc's reserves. Consequently, Heath argued against it vehemently, but was ultimately overridden by Tuckey, who had been instrumental in initiating the transaction. Heath remembers Tuckey explaining that the move was designed to 'even up the legs of the stool', a term he used to demonstrate the necessity for diversification to enhance stability, but Heath, Baylis and Martin in part interpreted this as a ploy by Tuckey to evade the resolution of the capital issue.

One of the primary reasons for Securities seeking more capital was so that it could embark upon proprietary trading. Proprietary trading was close to Heath's heart as he saw this as the means of funding continued expansion in the Nineties in the way that warrant trading had fuelled expansion in the Eighties. Proprietary trading was a business that was distinct from Securities' history in equity broking, in that, rather than soliciting and executing orders from clients, proprietary trading required the firm's employees to take risk using the company's capital, thereby generating revenues from their trading strategies, rather than through the commission paid by clients. Trading in newly listed futures and options, which Baring Securities Tokyo had started in 1988, had proved very successful in bad market conditions and Heath aggressively sought to expand this new derivative proprietary trading activity.

Baring Brothers was already involved in currency and debt trading, including foreign exchange, UK gilts and eurobonds, although under Michael Baring this activity had been limited and had shown very modest returns. Heath's desire to move into proprietary trading coincided with changes being made in the bank's treasury and trading operations. From the bank's point of view there was little point in the Barings' group investing in interest-rate trading activities, whether derivatives or cash market, in both the Brothers and the Securities. Besides, the bankers anticipated that the development of proprietary trading under Heath would be managed with the same perceived insouciance that warrant trading had been in the Eighties. They therefore wanted to ensure that any expansion of these activities came under their own management at the bank so that central controls could be established.

Heath was aware of the bank's point of view and made attempts to hire experienced professionals and to put in place such controls as he deemed necessary so that he could push ahead with his plans. He entered into lengthy negotiations with a team of proprietary traders from a US investment bank. Meanwhile, Andrew Baylis set Richard Johnston, an accountant who had been hired from Arthur Young and who, having just audited Bankers Trust's books, was one of the few people who understood derivatives at that time, to the task of setting up the firm's first risk control functions. However, Heath's plans to hire the team of traders ultimately fell through when Tuckey insisted that if they were to be hired at all it should be to work in the bank. Heath argues that the bank merely wanted the traders on their side of the fence so that the profits from the business would go on their own balance sheet to strengthen their weak business.

Heath and Baylis's attempts to placate the Brothers' concerns were largely futile because the bank's views as to Securities' ability to implement this kind of strategy professionally had reached such a low ebb. By this stage the bank's attitude was also being echoed within Securities. A senior director who departed in the early Nineties recalls that: 'Management was second-rate at best ... They had no concept of the words *risk* and *management* going together, for instance. The place was becoming unravelled.'

Heath's frustration over the Brothers' reluctance to provide additional capital and his knowledge that since the purchase of Dillon Read they no longer had it to give, ultimately led him to seek the money from outside the group. Heath insists that there had always been a gentleman's agreement that should the Brothers be unwilling or unable to provide the capital for expansion in future, Securities would have the option to seek an external partner. This was clearly not the way the Brothers understood the arrangement, so that when in 1992 Heath proposed that an external capital source be sought, a major debacle ensued with Tuckey. 'It was impracticable for the bank to consider that option as it would have signalled a massive retreat,' says a Hong Kong bank executive. 'In market terms the securities operation was driving the business. By that stage the tail was wagging the dog.'

Martin argues 'There is no question in my mind that financially it would have been better for the Barings Group at that time to have sold Baring Securities. They didn't have the wherewithal to take it forwards and we were on a path that required a lot more capital. We had the ability to achieve some pretty phenomenal growth. Any shareholder with an equity interest would have said it was the right thing to do, but because there was no shareholder in the normal sense [the Baring Foundation held the equity interest] we had no right of appeal.'

The banking executives told Heath that there was no way the broking arm could be sold in the state it was in, but indicated that they would be prepared to revisit this question in March 1993.

So long as Baring Securities maintained its remarkable profitability, Heath was almost invincible. However, when Baring Securities posted its results for 1992 his position was considerably undermined. The effects of the Japanese stock market collapse, the subsequent nose-dive in trading volumes, narrowing profit margins and the increased costs of continued expansion had pushed Baring Securities some £26 million into the red, the first loss in its eight-year history. While, according to Heath, the trading losses amounted to only £6 million, the fact that some £13 million of the total losses was money paid out in bonuses (which in all but a handful of instances were discretionary) was particularly difficult for the bank's executives to stomach. The result was met with surprise at Baring Securities. At the Brothers there was alarm: 'Suddenly there was a situation where Baring Securities was losing money, the markets were in retreat, and there was panic,' recalls a Brothers' corporate finance director.

The mood inside Baring Securities became sombre. Virtually all at senior management level in America Square and many senior executives overseas were seriously worried because they still had no idea what the company's real financial status was. This was brought to the attention of both Peter Baring and Andrew Tuckey by Peter Norris, a man who had a close affinity to Tuckey. Norris, a leading light in the corporate finance team who had been head of the bank's Hong Kong operation, had returned to London at the beginning of 1992 to formalize Equity Capital Markets, the first joint venture between Baring Brothers and Baring Securities to capitalize on the business that could be pursued between the corporate finance department in the bank and the brokers.

Tuckey insisted that Norris be given a mandate to review Baring Securities' affairs and make a formal report back to the Brothers' board with a view to formulating a new restructuring plan. Heath was forced to agree. His only consolation was that his ally Richard Greer had returned from Tokyo, where he had been Branch Manager, to work with Norris on the project, enabling Heath to have a daily report on the plans he and Norris were making.

Norris set to work immediately and made no secret of the fact that he was singularly unimpressed with most of the inner workings of Securities that he investigated from May to July of 1992. 'Norris discovered the absence of controls; there was no business plan or strategy, no effective control system or budgets, no management, offices had been opened all over the place. Christopher made all the decisions, trying to micro-manage it,' says one of Norris's colleagues from the bank. 'Baring Securities had outgrown itself. It was a classic case of the need for a new culture to be established from the previous freewheeling entrepreneurial entity.'

The report concluded, Norris was obliged to negotiate the plans for restructuring with the senior Securities players – Heath, Baylis, Martin, Kelly and Fraser – yet in reality they had little choice but to accept the plan. Under his proposal overall costs were to be reduced by 20 per cent within the following six months, staff were to be cut by 15 per cent, all European offices, with the exception of London and Paris, were to be closed down, the Australian operation was to be sold off, and warrant trading was to be virtually ceased, in all saving some £20 million. In return the Brothers would put in a cash injection of £45 million. Baring Brothers and Baring Securities were to be merged within three years to create an integrated investment bank.

Even before Norris had produced his final report, there could have been little doubt in anyone's mind that it was one of the Brothers' primary intentions to significantly restructure the top management of Baring Securities. Seeing the writing on the wall, top executives, including those who had been members of Heath's old guard, began to switch political alliance, and the speed with which some of Heath's former allies changed sides has left long-standing resentment between the two factions.

At the end of September 1992, Norris was installed as Chief Operating Officer. The Baring Securities Management Committee of five was disbanded and replaced by a new committee of seventeen members, including regional branch managers. While the company had obviously grown to a size where broader management was required, the sudden opportunity for self-advancement opened up by this expansion of the Management Committee engendered a level of factional in-fighting that was unprecedented in a company which had been unusually free of internal politics. 'It made the place a political hotbed,' Heath remembers. 'The Management Committee became a battleground. It was an opportunity for people to snipe at each other rather than actually managing the business. Although the committee had expanded overnight, there were people who hadn't been included in that seventeen who felt they had been neglected and so were angling to get on it. It opened up a Pandora's box of people's ambitions and politicking. People took their focus off what they were supposed to be doing on a day-to-day basis because they saw an opportunity for management and the chance for profit share offered by membership of the committee, and they decided that they wanted to get on the gravy train. In the past it hadn't been on the agenda, because the door wasn't open.' The uncertainty and lack of confidence during this period caused a number of people to become uncharacteristically aggressive and stimulated dissent and political in-fighting at all levels. As a former London director described it, 'the company had become a nest of vipers.'

The restructuring began immediately after Norris's arrival. In late October over one hundred staff were axed; the majority of businesses were kept whole but were scaled back, with most of the lay-offs coming from non-professional staff. Heath relinquished his post as Chief Executive Officer of Securities and was temporarily moved upstairs to assume the position of Chairman, thus all but removing him from the restructuring process. At that stage, Heath offered to resign: 'If that was the direction they wanted to go in, effectively taking control by the back door, then I wanted to leave.' Peter Baring later said that plans were being formulated at that stage to change the management structure, but since no firm decision had been taken he continued to reassure Heath, as did other top executives, that they wanted him to stay.

Management insensitivity prevailed even in the way that staff received their notice. A list of people to be fired was drawn up and given to the security guards. Upon arrival at work, each person's name was checked against the list and, if it appeared there, they were escorted to a meeting room which quickly became over-crowded with concerned and expectant employees. Over the course of the following hour they were extracted one by one and given the option of leaving immediately or spending half an hour over a cup of tea with a recruitment consultant in the next room. Unexpectedly for him, the person who had typed up the original list found when he arrived at work that morning that his name had been added to it.

Despite the cutbacks of October, it was clear by the spring that further reductions were needed and there was growing trepidation amongst the employees that significant management changes would take place. In March, further cuts combined with the departure of a number of employees fearful that they had no future within the company brought the total to over 200, representing approximately 10 per cent of the work force.

On the evening of Saturday, 14 March 1993, Heath received a call from Peter Baring summoning him to a meeting the following morning – the Ides of March. That Sunday, Baring, Tuckey and Heath met at the Brothers offices at 8 Bishopsgate. Heath says he was told that a new management team was needed and that, as his presence would inhibit its operational abilities, his resignation was required. That famous question 'Et tu, Brute?' even floated around the table, though the overall tone was civilized and amicable. One observer said at the time: 'We have never had anything remotely like the sort of blinding rows you hear about at other places.'

Heath recalls being shown a pre-prepared press release to all City editors that cited disagreement about strategic policy as the reason for his departure. Also on the list were Andrew Baylis, Ian Martin, Vanessa Gibson (a senior manager who was close to Baylis), and Jim Reed (Branch Manager of the New York operation).

In the wake of these departures, senior management was restructured. The new management board was headed by Peter Norris, who was appointed Chief Executive, while Andrew Fraser and Diarmaid Kelly were appointed joint Deputy Chairmen. Miles Rivett-Carnac, the former head of Baring Asset Management, came out of retirement to assume the role of Chairman and to act as advisor to Peter Norris. As if to demonstrate that the camaraderie of earlier days hadn't gone out of the door with those that had left, one trader's response to Miles Rivett-Carnac's appointment was to nickname him 'Mine's a large Cognac', a sobriquet that Rivett-Carnac delighted in and turned to his own humorous use on many occasions.

The changes were bold, dramatic and potentially destabilizing. It is perhaps testament to the employees' loyalty to the company, which owed much to the team spirit nurtured by Heath and to their belief in the future of the business itself, that, despite the low level of morale, the company did not fall apart immediately. However, to most, Norris was an unknown entity both personally and professionally. This engendered an erosion of confidence and faith, resulting in a feeling of vulnerability amongst most of the staff who no longer felt sure of their standing within the company; the period is referred to as 'the Turbulence' by many. Even on the new Management Committee it was clear that Norris, at least for now, held all the cards.

7 | Betting on the Future

'Far from having won the jewel in the crown, he had in fact
unwittingly grasped a poisoned chalice.'

While Heath and Norris were embroiled in their battle over the
future direction of Baring Securities, Nick and Lisa Leeson, on the
other side of the world in sunny Singapore, were settling into their
new ex-pat life. While Lisa was making a new home for them,
her husband was busy establishing the accounting and settlement
functions for Barings' new indirect subsidiary, Baring Futures
(Singapore) Pte Ltd, for which his experience in the London back
office served him well.

Leeson's knowledge and experience of futures and options trading and settlement had, since his arrival in Baring Securities in
1989, grown at a similar pace to that of most other employees
in the firm. Futures and options were new to almost all of the
predominantly British and Japanese staff and managers, myself
included, and we all had to learn rapidly once the firm began trading
in the instruments in 1988. The company hired professionals in
the field to set up the derivatives business, but for the majority at
Barings the learning was hands-on. The development of Leeson's,
my own and other staff members' expertise in this area equally
reflected the development of the markets themselves, because the
late Eighties and early Nineties were a watershed period for the
derivatives markets in Asia. To understand what Leeson and Baring
Securities were doing during this formative period, it helps to know
a little about the background and workings of the markets in which
the company became involved.

Commodity futures markets began in the US over a hundred
years ago to help merchants and farmers reduce the impact that
price fluctuations had on the profitability of their businesses. A fruit

farmer in Florida who grows oranges, for example, has a lot of fixed costs in running his business and does not want to have to speculate on what the final cash price for his crop will be after harvest. By selling frozen orange juice futures, a clearly comparable proxy to his fresh orange crop, he can lock in now a known sale price for his future crop. If there is a bumper crop and prices fall, the profit from his futures contract will offset the reduced price of his cash crop; if there is a weak harvest and prices rise, he will lose money on his futures contracts but secure a high price for his cash crop.

The trading of financial futures contracts based on financial instruments instead of commodities commenced in 1971 with the introduction of foreign currency contracts, followed in 1975 by what have become the most successful contracts in history: interest rate futures. As a result of two OPEC oil crises, the establishment of the European Monetary System, large-scale Latin American debt rescheduling and wildly gyrating US dollar exchange rates and interest rates, the Seventies and early Eighties were turbulent years for financial markets worldwide. Investors, corporates, traders, even governments, flocked to use the new futures markets to help them hedge against the currency, interest-rate, oil, gold, or other price fluctuations that affected their businesses. The remarkable growth in futures markets over these years resulted as much from their use by speculators as by hedgers, but for both the attractions of futures were the same. Futures provide standardized contracts, a visible exchange, guaranteed settlement through a central clearing house and – perhaps most important of all – the need to pay only a small portion of the total value of a position up front. This initial payment is referred to as margin and additional payments, or maintenance margin, are only required if the market does not move in favour of the investor.

Futures and options had long been traded and widely used by investors in the US, but the Asian markets for such products were still in a comparatively immature phase in the late Eighties and early Nineties. During this period they underwent dramatic changes with the opening of new exchanges, the setting up of new contracts, the education of a vast number of investors who were new to derivatives, and the introduction and swift growth of arbitrage trading.

The Singapore government opened the Singapore International Monetary Exchange (SIMEX) in September 1984, the first futures and options exchange of its kind in the region, as a further step towards its goal of establishing the island as Asia's foremost financial centre. It took the Chicago Mercantile Exchange (CME), one of the US's most pre-eminent exchanges, as its role model, in particular adopting the margining system it had developed, known by its mnemonic SPAN (Standard Portfolio Analysis of Risk). SIMEX successfully co-pioneered the world's first mutual offset trading system with the CME. This international trading link heralded the world's first step towards a 24-hour trading system across different time zones, enabling Eurodollar futures, for instance, to be traded on one exchange and then transferred or liquidated at the other exchange, while the investor only has to pay margin on his combined positions. SIMEX, like the CME and the majority of futures and options markets, is an open-outcry market, where all orders, whether for clients or for the company's own account, are executed in a trading pit.

In September 1986 SIMEX launched the world's first Japanese stock index futures based on the Nikkei 225 stock index, the most popular quoted stock index in Japan. It was to be another two years before futures markets got the green light in Japan, where long-awaited financial deregulation had been bogged down amidst political procrastination, but finally on 9 September 1988 the Japanese Nikkei 225 futures contracts debuted on the Osaka Securities Exchange (OSE). At the same time, the competing Tokyo Stock Exchange (TSE) launched a futures contract on TOPIX (Tokyo Stock Price Index), the second most popular stock index.

The new onshore futures contracts sparked the interest of both the Japanese financial community and foreign securities companies with a presence in Japan, with the result that in the first year, trading volume in the contracts exceeded the most wild expectations. The new contracts also added a whole new dimension to the opportunities for arbitrage in Japanese stocks. Proprietary trading at the primary US investment banks rapidly spread from simple stock/futures arbitrage – buying one and selling the other in order to profit from perceived temporary mispricings, while assuming little or no market direction risk – to a broader range of strategies encompassing SIMEX, the TSE and OSE. Consequently, trading activity in the Nikkei 225 contracts on SIMEX was boosted.

As profits from warrant trading at Baring Securities still remained buoyant throughout the late Eighties, Heath showed little interest in the early developments on SIMEX, but could not ignore the potential of the futures markets once it was clear that local contracts were to open in Osaka and Tokyo. Mike Killian, a moustached native of Chicago who raised eyebrows in an English company for wearing black Reeboks with his suits at work, was one of the first to bring Heath's attention to the potential of these markets. Killian, who was then general manager of the futures and options group at Chase Manhattan Bank in Singapore, approached Heath in 1986, with a proposal whereby Chase would execute all of Baring Securities' potential futures and options business on SIMEX. Although this proved of little interest to Heath at the time, Killian maintained contact with him and was the first to receive a call when Heath decided to take the initial steps to build a futures and options agency brokerage business at Baring Securities in Japan, by which Barings would generate revenue from the commission it charged clients for executing their orders.

Killian had touched the nerve that triggered Heath's change of heart. By late 1988 the Nikkei 225 index was roaring on up towards the 40,000 level, amidst increasing concerns about an impending crash. The US investment banks that Baring Securities was leading in the competition for equity brokerage business, had already established futures and options brokerage teams. If the market did collapse as many predicted and investors sought to protect their portfolios by using futures and options, Barings could lose substantial equity business because it was unable to offer clients a professional broking service in both futures and cash equity products. Heath became convinced that, even if the market didn't fall, there was a prime opportunity to market futures and options to the large number of Barings' existing, renowned, global clients, many of whom had a strong focus on Japan.

Killian joined Baring Securities Tokyo at the beginning of September 1988 to head up the new department. Shortly afterwards he was joined by Su Khoo, a Malaysian actuary and mathematician, and Bruce Benson, an American, who had both been recruited in London by Andrew Baylis. As the firm did not have a seat on SIMEX to begin with, Killian used his old firm Chase Manhattan to execute most of the new business on the Exchange.

Heath wanted to market the new derivative products to his existing clients, but in practice the team found that Barings' traditional clients put up a considerable resistance to using futures and options as part of their investment strategies, regardless of the market's performance. This was largely because of their lack of familiarity with, and consequent caution about, dealing in the new instruments. Killian was therefore forced to utilize his US securities firm contacts to seek the necessary order flow to get the new business off the ground.

In June 1989, some nine months after the setting up of the agency brokerage business, Baring Securities opened an office in Osaka, the centre for Nikkei 225 futures trading, and decided to begin trading in options using the firm's own capital. Su Khoo assumed the role of proprietary trader and established an options trading book in Tokyo. Khoo was eager to leave the agency broking business run by Killian both because her personality and talents were better suited to trading on an individual basis, and because she and Killian had not proved particularly compatible. Although Khoo had left the original team, they all remained in close proximity in the office due to the synergies between the two businesses, so relations were a little strained between her and Killian. To bridge the communication gap, Fred Hochberger, who had helped pioneer the firm's warrant and convertible bond research, and had the market knowledge, experience and tact required to fulfil this combined trading and sales role, set himself up as liaison between Khoo's proprietary trading book and Killian's clients. Hochberger went on to become the star of Killian's sales team, branching out to set up and run the futures and options broking operations in Hong Kong.

Khoo's trading strategies were at first neutral to market direction, but relied upon market movement, taking positions that would profit from a change in the market's volatility. As time went on and confidence grew, the positioning became bolder until at the end of 1990, the book realized a dramatic increase in profitability through a combination of directional and volatility trading. Heath was ecstatic as it suddenly opened the window of opportunity he needed and offered potential salvation from the dispute with Baring Brothers over the sustainability of profits from warrant trading. The profits were all the more sweet to him for having been made as the Tokyo market was falling.

Although Heath enjoyed the new-found revenues, the development of Khoo's trading operation created an unexpected dilemma because Heath's 'client is king' approach to the world was suddenly thrown into question as the proprietary or 'house account' trading of futures and options began to draw complaints from the agency broking operation and their clients. Many clients felt that there was a conflict of interest between proprietary trading and agency broking businesses within the same firm, as they assumed that the execution of orders for the internal trading books would take preference over their own orders. This assumption was largely misconceived, as the placing of house orders ahead of client orders in hand at the same price, a trading practice known as 'front running', is not permitted on any exchange.

In fact Baring Securities futures and options team in Tokyo had maintained a Chinese wall between the two departments from the outset. The agency business ran the trading floor and settlement operations, while Khoo had the option of dealing with Killian's agency arm – where she was treated as just another customer – or with another broker. Khoo therefore appropriately competed with Barings' external clients in the execution of orders in the same way that the clients competed with each other in the market as a whole. The problem lay not in how Baring Securities had set up the two businesses internally, but in how the firm's development into proprietary trading was perceived externally by the clients and in the way the agency broking team had marketed their services in the past. Killian and his team had always used the firm's *lack* of proprietary trading activities as a key sales pitch. Unlike such US competitors as Morgan Stanley or Salomon Brothers, which were comparably large players in the markets, Barings transacted a similar scale of business, but uniquely that business was drawn almost exclusively from external client orders, whereas the US houses' proprietary trading activities contributed substantially to their overall business on the Exchange.

Indeed, many of Baring Securities' clients had switched from leading US firms with longer histories in the derivatives markets, to Baring Securities because they felt they might not be getting a fair deal with the broker they had been using before due to the scale of the US firm's proprietary trading activities. In reality, clients dealt with Baring Securities because of the professional quality of the service and the conscientiousness and personalities of those that provided it, but it was not in Barings' interest to play down its competitors' biggest disadvantage. This disadvantage and client misconception came back to plague Baring Securities' marketing efforts on futures and options broking as their own proprietary trading activities gradually increased.

It was this factor above all which, despite the strict separation of the businesses in Tokyo, and later in Hong Kong under the leadership of Hochberger, led to friction within the firm between the two departments, friction which grew in proportion to the expansion of proprietary trading.

By 1992 an increasing amount of Baring Securities' client business in futures and options was moving offshore from Japan to Singapore, driven by the increased restrictions imposed by the Ministry of Finance on futures markets in Japan in an attempt to minimize the effects of index arbitrage that the authorities believed was pushing the Japanese stock market down. These restrictions, combined with the American clients' preference for open-outcry markets and the substantially cheaper commissions required by

SIMEX, gave a dramatic boost to SIMEX's market share of Nikkei 225 futures business.

As Barings' business on SIMEX increased, it made economic sense for Barings to become a member of the Exchange itself, rather than continuing to pay broking commissions to Chase Manhattan which was still executing the majority of its business there. To begin with, Andrew Baylis was reluctant to give the go-ahead for this SIMEX seat, but when Killian, Hochberger and Benson told him they were going to buy the seat themselves, he finally agreed that Barings should purchase it. Once the legal documentation for the new firm had been established and the capital requirements organized, Nick Leeson was posted to Singapore to establish the accounting and settlements operations of Baring Futures, an indirect subsidiary of Baring Securities Limited that had a seat on SIMEX and employed its own floor staff. Leeson hired a local floor trader to execute Barings' trades in the pit and a handful of back office staff to help him. The operation was run in the same way as any other execution centre, Barings' floor trader simply executing orders relayed to the floor by colleagues in Tokyo and Osaka, and the back office settling them.

Leeson's reporting lines were not clearly defined or, it would seem, adequately understood from the start. The Bank of England inquiry team received conflicting testimonies as to who was responsible for Leeson for much of his time in Singapore. Baring Securities and Baring Futures were located in the same Singapore office block but occupied different premises, served by different lifts. Both the Regional Manager and the Regional Operations Manager (Bax and Jones respectively) had their offices on the 24th floor. Leeson, when not on the SIMEX floor, worked in the Baring Futures office on the 14th floor. Baring Futures (Singapore) was run as a separate operation from Baring Securities, although Bax and Jones had local responsibility for operational matters and were both directors of the new company. There was clearly communication and contact between Leeson and Jones, and Leeson and Bax, however both Jones and Bax were more focused on Baring Securities than Baring Futures. Since the bank's crash, both Bax and Jones have said that

Leeson did not report to them on the trades he carried out on SIMEX.

Barings was a relative latecomer to the eight-year-old Singapore market, making its debut when more than three hundred firms already traded there. SIMEX is big in Asia, but it is not large on a global scale; although it traded 24 million futures contracts in 1994 it is still relatively small compared to LIFFE in London or the large US exchanges. When it began trading on SIMEX, Baring Securities' presence was virtually invisible, dwarfed as it was by the large US investment houses such as Morgan Stanley that then dominated the market.

As in Jakarta and London, Leeson proved himself efficient in his new capacity of floor manager and head of the SIMEX operation. As with all start-up operations, Baring Securities had encountered a number of problems in the settlement of its derivatives trades, to which internal memos from this period bear witness. For instance, a 15 November 1991 memorandum from Ian Martin to Mike Killian in Tokyo recorded six complaints from clients that day concerning problems in settling transactions on their behalf. Leeson set up the settlements and accounting departments efficiently and established himself as a godsend in the eyes of Killian's agency broking team in Tokyo because he could always be relied upon to ensure that any such discrepancies over executions or mismatched trades would be sorted out promptly. Indeed, he seemed invaluable in sorting out such issues, his success leading to such comments as Mike Killian's 'We need ten more Nicks', in response to Ian Martin's memo. Killian described Leeson as 'leading the current rescue effort'.

Before his first year in Singapore was up, Leeson put in a request to take the SIMEX examinations so he could wear a badge on the floor of the Exchange. He passed these exams in late 1992 and at about the same time he was appointed General Manager of Baring Futures (Singapore). When he applied for this trading licence, SIMEX, which had no direct contact with the Securities and Futures Authority in London, was unaware that his application for a licence to trade in London had been rejected. Leeson clearly had ambitions to trade himself, but at this point the idea of having a trading badge was that he would be able to accompany visiting clients on a tour of the Exchange's trading floor and talk to them directly about what was happening in the market, as well as entertaining them in the evening. 'It made sense,' says Mike Killian. 'Having an extra badge on the floor and another person in the booth made us look more respectable. Nick could give clients a tour of the floor and it helped them to be able to call someone on the floor that they knew personally to ask about the market.' By the end of 1992 Leeson was the proud wearer of a gold-and-navy striped jacket, Baring Futures' trading colours.

This, however, was to prove a fatal mistake. Leeson was still in charge of the settlements and accounting department of Baring Futures, but now had the ability to trade too. Indeed, before the end of 1992, he had begun executing client orders on SIMEX for Killian's agency broking team in Tokyo. To give someone the ability to both execute orders and settle them is rather like making a poacher into a game-keeper.

The only point at which both proprietary and agency broking business streams converge is on the exchange floor or dealing-room screen. The Osaka Securities Exchange employs a screen-based execution system, by which all orders are entered into the system and automatically matched by a central computer, subject to a set of rules predetermined by the exchange. On SIMEX, an open-outcry market, the floor traders execute an order, passed down to them by telephone from their colleagues in the office, by standing in a designated area, or pit, and shouting out the details of the order until another trader agrees to match their bid or offer. Orders passed to the floor are accompanied by instructions to the trader on how they are to be executed; sometimes the trader will have full discretion, while on other occasions he will have to follow a rigid format. In addition to simply executing orders, it is common for experienced traders in an open-outcry market to have the authority to trade for profit on behalf of the company, committing the firm's capital.

In his new capacity as floor trader for Killian's agency broking team, Leeson was essentially just a middle man, carrying out the orders relayed to him from the office according to the specifications given. As he had no previous trading experience, he was not at first given any discretion as to how to execute these orders. Nevertheless, his continued command of the back office meant that he had, in effect, an open opportunity to abuse his position, since he now had the ability to fudge the accounts for the trades he had done.

Leeson soon proved himself as a seemingly able floor trader. His executions of client orders appeared to be good and he was popular with the clients he dealt with over the phone and entertained when they were in Singapore. He continued to run the back office settlement functions of the company efficiently too. Leeson's desire to please everyone may well have been the reason why he began to take advantage of his position as head of both settlements and trading. A member of the futures and options broking team called Leeson the 'please, please me man', pointing out that, 'He was on his own. He didn't seem to realize that the markets didn't allow for pleasing all the people all of the time.'

By the time Leeson had made it on to the trading floor in 1992, Baring Securities' proprietary trading operation had developed considerably from the option trading book originally set up by Khoo. The option volatility trading book had been producing volatile results, so attention had turned to index arbitrage – trading in baskets of stock and index futures that replicate each other to benefit from temporary pricing anomalies. In autumn 1990 when the Tokyo market spiked up 2000 points in one day and the futures were suspended with buyers only, Killian was asked by a client at a US investment bank to purchase approximately 20,000 shares of each of the components of the Nikkei 225. It was the biggest stock order that Baring Securities had ever received at that time and when Killian approached the head equity trader to confirm whether it was feasible, the response was: 'What? You must be joking?' Baring Securities succeeded in executing the order, but problems with this execution and the settlement of the trade almost caused it to fail, which would potentially have left the Tokyo operation in a very difficult financial situation.

Naturally reluctant to pass up such lucrative business, but equally concerned about the settlement risk of such large trades, Securities management agreed to place greater emphasis on expanding the capability of the index arbitrage book. Richard Johnston, who had been recruited by Baylis to set up the firm's first risk control function, was set to the task with the assistance of Fernando Gueler, a young Californian computer wizard who had proved his mathematical skills in the Tokyo research department. Under Johnston's guidance, Baring Securities preceded to sink millions of pounds into new computer systems over the next few years that gradually automated a great deal of the execution process in the equity markets and constantly tracked the many variables to provide second by second analysis of outstanding trades and positions. The new system became widely used by clients as well as Johnston's trading team, providing income flow for Killian's crew as well as benefiting the company's increasingly profitable index arbitrage activities.

This business grew through 1993 as arbitrage opportunities between the Nikkei 225 contracts in Osaka and those on SIMEX increased, and so the Tokyo team needed a counterpart in Singapore to execute their orders there. Leeson was in the best position to conduct such business from the trading floor of SIMEX, having immediate access to SIMEX trading pits and almost instant access over the squawk box to his colleagues at dealing terminals for the Japanese exchanges. Having proved himself adept at conducting transactions for Killian's agency broking team, he was given the job. 'Nick had been talking to the boys in Tokyo and there had been a lot of bonding, so it made sense to let him do it,' says Mike Killian. 'He cut his teeth on it and became very adept at it quite quickly. After a while he was doing a pretty good job. He wasn't just moving positions from Osaka to SIMEX, but sometimes back again.' Over the next few months Leeson appeared to become more and more proficient at handling these executions for the index arbitrage team and was given an increasing amount of discretion with the orders. By mid-August 1994 Leeson had been given his own Nikkei arbitrage trading book, which was booked in Baring Securities Japan on the basis of the information sent each evening from

Singapore. This index arbitrage or so-called 'switching' activity became known as 'Leeson's business'. As both Barings' proprietary trading business and that for clients developed, Leeson hired another half a dozen settlements staff and traders respectively to help him.

While the proprietary trading business developed, a broader conflict arose within Baring Securities regarding its ultimate objective and the purpose of its development within the company. Heath had perceived proprietary trading merely as a means to an end; it replaced the diminishing profitability of warrant trading to pay for the cost of expansion. Norris, appearing on the scene in 1992, took a different view. While both saw it as a good revenue source, Norris wanted the proprietary trading team to work more closely with other departments, sharing valuable financial information to make the business as a whole more competitive. For example, individuals who had their fingers on the pulse of the markets and excellent information sources could be used to greater advantage by the corporate finance team when pricing new issues. Norris described it as 'one leg of a stool', a phrase highly reminiscent of Tuckey.

When Norris took control of Baring Securities, his plan for the overall direction of the company naturally encompassed the development of proprietary trading. Norris noted that the equity derivatives business of Baring Securities was not working effectively as a group nor did there seem to be much culture or sympathy for the business in the firm as a whole.

Futures and options activities had been established within Baring Securities back in 1989 under the banner of Japanese Equity Product. Consequently, as trading operations developed in Japan and other derivatives activities were initiated in other parts of the world, a collection of disparate sales and trading teams and individuals had grown up in various centres with little or no global strategy and no central management. The situation was exacerbated because on recruitment, derivatives personnel all too often discovered that their role was insufficiently defined. From 1990 to 1993 there was a whole string of people in trading, sales and research of warrants, CBs, futures and options who were based in London, Hong Kong, Tokyo and New York who found that their mandates constantly overlapped. Members of the derivatives group called this the 'Divide and Rule' policy. This business fell into the domain of first Andrew Baylis and then Ian Martin in late 1992, but the role of acting head of the unruly derivatives group was offered to a series of individuals who Baylis, Heath and Martin felt comfortable with. However, those individuals often proved to lack sufficient experience or were not given the necessary authority or support to fulfil the task, which became a hopeless endeavour. One former executive estimates that there were more than half a dozen heads of global equity derivatives in Baring Securities over a two-year period, a turnover rate so high that soon nobody was taken too seriously in the position as they were not expected to last long.

In retrospect, Heath acknowledges that the management of the derivatives operation lacked co-ordination. 'We should have hired someone out of a US bank to run that side of the business,' he reflects. 'Although it might have appeared disparate to the outside world, and to some inside, it actually ran very well and very profitably, but it could have done with more strategic direction than it had.'

What this lack of co-ordination was to prove ultimately, however, was that during this period there was no continued central management of Nick Leeson's operation in Singapore. Although Leeson worked as a head of execution on SIMEX both for Mike Killian's broking operation and for the index arbitrage team in Tokyo, there was never a strict hierarchy. 'The reporting line was always very confusing,' says a member of the agency broking team. 'A lot of times it wasn't clear who was in charge of him or who was supposed to watch over him.' While some believed that Leeson reported to Killian for his agency execution business, Killian has stated that he thought Leeson was 'under the watchful eye ... of the Singapore branch'. To all intents and purposes Leeson was left to his own devices.

Having noted by mid-1993 both the haphazard way in which the business had developed and the fact that culturally it did not seem to fit into the firm, Norris felt that the derivatives business needed a strong-minded individual to co-ordinate it globally or he would have to consider closing it down. His solution was to bring in Ron Baker from the bank to take charge of Baring Securities' derivatives proprietary trading in October 1993.

Baker, an Australian, had been an unusual choice for Baring Brothers. A strongly opinionated ex-hippy and Pavarotti look-alike, he at first seemed something of a misfit in the staid banking halls of Barings. He wore gingham shirts and brightly coloured Swatch watches, which he made a habit of giving away on overseas trips when he would replace them at the airport. But perhaps Baker's most novel characteristic was the fact that he was one of the first senior bank staff to sport a beard. In Heath's day a number of people who had experimented with facial hair were swiftly encouraged to remove it, as Heath was known to have a strong aversion to beards, often citing the maxim: 'never trust a man with a beard'. However, even if Baker had been around in Heath's era, he was clearly not a character to have been persuaded to change his mind about such a thing.

A member of Baker's Financial Products Group recalls an evening out with his boss in a high-class French restaurant during a team conference in Bruges, one of the restaurant capitals of the world. The group arrived at the restaurant ravenous after their pre-dinner drinks, and Baker asked if he could order something that was not on the menu, to which the waiter replied, 'Certainly sir.' Baker requested a beefburger but was told that the restaurant could not oblige. 'But you said I could have anything. You must have some beef,' he insisted. When the waiter continued to resist, Baker paid him to go out to McDonalds to fetch a burger, which he promptly did, unwrapping it in the kitchen and serving it up to him on a plate.

Baker had been hired by Michael Baring, at the time Head of Treasury and Trading in the bank, in January 1992, following the debacle with Heath over proprietary trading and just a couple of months before Nick Leeson was sent to Singapore. He had previously been head of Eurobonds at Bankers Trust, an acknowledged leader in the field of high-tech derivatives expertise, although Baker himself had been involved in the low-tech side of the business. He was given the task of building up an emerging market debt business for Baring Brothers & Co., which was based in London with satellites in New York and Tokyo.

Baker's team grew swiftly. He was joined in June 1992 by Mary Walz, a sharp-minded American woman from Michigan with whom he had worked at Bankers Trust London. Over the next six months more than half a dozen other former BT employees were to join Baker at Brothers, giving rise to an in-house joke that the company should be renamed Barings Trust. Indeed, by 1995 there were approximately fifty emigres from BT at Barings, lured by Baker who had sold them on the idea of Barings' business plans and the lack of political interference in fulfilling these plans which was something many of them had encountered at BT. Despite the team's expansion, however, it was soon apparent that the emerging markets debt business was both volatile and would take time to develop so Baker sought other areas for the team to expand into that would provide a more immediate and stable revenue base and help finance the growth of the emerging markets business. This he achieved in part by developing a credit-trading business supported by an asset-swap linkup with the newly formed Abbey National Baring Derivatives. However, when approached by Norris in mid-1993 to also take control of Baring Securities equity derivative operations, Baker considered it an opportunity too good to miss, as the profitability of Securities' index arbitrage business in Tokyo immediately solved a number of shorter term financing questions which were constraining the growth of his debt business.

As far as Norris was concerned, the decision to place the equity derivatives business under Baker's management was taken for three reasons: it did not fit easily within the culture of the Securities broking business and there was no client overlap; the Debt Financial Products Group Baker had been running since he joined the bank had experience of proprietary trading; and Baker had the management skills to motivate the proprietary traders. The futures and options agency sales business under Killian in Tokyo remained outside Baker's responsibility at that time.

Given the lack of confidence and feeling of vulnerability among Securities' employees after the period of turbulence surrounding Heath's departure in March 1993, particularly those in the derivatives businesses, in addition to the fact that Baker and his colleagues' lacked experience in equity markets and the agency broking of derivatives, it was not surprising that Norris received a number of calls from irritated and frustrated employees questioning Baker's appointment. The members of the futures and options agency broking department, anticipating that Baker would eventually be put in charge of their own operation, were particularly worried about whether Norris understood the conflict of interest between the proprietary trading and the agency broking businesses. Norris's response to such complaints was reportedly: 'Ron Baker has never not delivered anything to the bank he's promised and I'm sure he's the right candidate for the job.'

Baker's age and maturity meant that he was better able to represent the group at top management level, rather than being, as his predecessors in the post had, forced to seek support through political alliance with senior managers who did not necessarily have the derivative group's interest at heart. His strong personality and his policy of going out for beers with his boys and looking after them, won him many friends from within his new group: 'He was a master of the hearts and minds game,' says one of the debt traders who had followed him to Barings from BT. However, Baker also made many enemies in other quarters due to his brash, uncompromising views and because he was not prepared to suffer fools gladly.

On his first visit to Hong Kong in 1994 since taking over the equity derivatives business, Baker went out for dinner at one of Hong Kong's top restaurants with some of his new team. The waiter who served the party irritated them throughout the evening with his ineptitude at taking and delivering their orders. Their frustration mounted to such a degree that Baker was moved to get up from the table, seize the waiter by the lapels of his jacket and tell him what he thought of him. At this the whole restaurant broke into loud cheers and vigorous applause as they too had had their appetites dulled by the waiter's hopelessness and were thankful that someone had finally registered a suitably forceful complaint.

Baker moved quickly to try and rationalize the group of some thirty individuals worldwide that he had inherited at Securities into a cohesive, focused group which could assume a strong identity and a more professional stance. The new team was called the Financial Products Group, the first department within Barings to straddle the banking and broking operations. It was made up of three key businesses. The Securities equity derivative department was subsumed by a new operation known as the Structured Products Group, later renamed Equity Financial Products Group. The other two were: Emerging Market Debt Trading (Latin America, Asia etc.) and Debt Financial Products (asset swaps and credit trading). Baker placed three of his key ex-Bankers Trust colleagues in charge of the three core business groups: Mary Walz headed up SPG, Mike Tomms DFP and Mark Fisher EMD.

In order to further unite his new teams, Baker introduced regular 'off-sites' at Barings. The concept of 'off-sites' – seminar weekends held in hotels – was developed by US investment banks and was a practice Baker and some of his team had grown accustomed to at Bankers Trust. During such weekends there would be daytime conferences during which the FPG's strategy and product development were discussed and targets for future business set, the profitability of which was expected to cover the cost of the weekend. Given that many of Baker's team were new to one another, the evening dinners and drinks proved to be considerable bonding sessions.

The linch-pin in profitability for the equity derivatives group was the Tokyo arbitrage trading book set up by Johnston and Gueler. There had been a number of staff changes in this department, as there had been in many others; in 1992 both Johnston and Khoo returned to London to pursue new job mandates (though both left the company during the Turbulence when these positions proved untenable). However, the team under the new leadership of Fernando Gueler had continued to post good profits, profits which had been steadily increasing over the preceding 12–18 months. The scale and stability of the earnings of this business made it appear to many to be the jewel in the crown of Baring Securities. Baker and Walz were therefore keen to win the support and following of the team of young and relatively impressionable traders who were currently in charge of that operation. Although Leeson was reportedly not on the original list of roughly thirty employees which Baker inherited in October 1993, his role on the SIMEX trading floor meant that he was closely associated with the Tokyo arbitrage team.

Since the bank's crash there has been much disagreement as to who Leeson reported to from the period after Baker's take-over of the Securities derivatives proprietary trading group in October 1993. During 1994, on a product basis, Norris, Walz and Gueler believed that Leeson reported through the management chain (Gueler and Walz) to Baker as head of the Financial Products Group. Baker told the Bank of England investigators: 'There was a lot of ambiguity about where Nick sat during 1994 . . . De facto without knowing it, I inherited the income stream and the trading strategy that Nick was pursuing from 1 January 1994 . . . I did not feel that Nick reported to me, or that I had any real organizational control over him until the second half of 1994.'

The high level of reported profitability and consequent prestige enjoyed by the equity derivatives group meant that control of it was coveted and aggressively sought by other senior individuals. The fact that Baker had stepped in from outside the securities arm and been handed the jewel in the crown as part of his increasingly broad responsibility for all derivatives activities, drew jealous attacks and criticism from many quarters.

Baker was handed control of it as he was far more able than his rivals to articulate a longer term plan for a broad variety of proprietary trading activities that would enable Barings as a whole to diversify their risks and produce more sustainable earnings. Baker's talent at painting this longer-term global picture led him to assuming responsibility not only for Baring Securities' derivative trading activities, but also for the futures and options agency broking business.

Due to the long-standing sensitivity of the futures and options broking team to proprietary trading, there was a natural reluctance on their part to have their lot thrown in with the rest of Baker's team which included the trading side. In the light of their concerns that Baker had no feel for the natural business conflict between the two businesses, they assumed that Baker would use the agency broking business to benefit the proprietary trading books, by allowing the proprietary traders to see what the clients were doing and use that information to profit themselves.

By this time their attitude verged on mistrust, as is exemplified in one member's comment that: 'Peter Norris allowed Ron Baker to be in charge of agency broking and proprietary trading, so the two sides of the Chinese wall became fudged. You can't have both agency broking and proprietary trading reporting to one line; it should only happen at the highest board level. If it happens downstream you've got a problem. Norris gave the fox the key to the hen house.' In fact, the logistics and controls of the way the operation was set up under Baker were not uncommon in broking terms, given that Baker was a senior officer of the bank. Again the agency broking team's arguments merely reflected their paranoia about the fact that they thought the clients would not deal with them if they were considered to be associated with proprietary trading.

Nevertheless, this relatively insignificant sideshow got top billing, drawing attention away from the fact that the *real* conflict of interest still lay in the fact that Leeson was head of settlements while his trading activities on behalf of both clients and the index arbitrage team in Tokyo had burgeoned. This situation had existed since 1992 and his opportunities for abusing it had simply grown as his own trading activities increased.

Despite the internal resistance from the agency group to his takeover of all derivatives activities, Baker was stimulated by his expanded franchise and the increased scope of influence it brought him. He was soon to discover, however, that in ultimately securing control of Baring Securities' equity derivatives operations, far from having won the jewel in the crown, he had in fact unwittingly grasped a poisoned chalice.

8 | One Mutant Cell

'It was the perfect environment for cancer to grow rapidly.'
TRADER, BARING SECURITIES, TOKYO

The restructuring process which began under Norris's guidance in September of 1992 was progressive and much needed, but it naturally engendered confusion amongst top management and muddled reporting lines and there were dangers inherent in the sheer pace of change. Rather as a lobster changing its shell is left open to attack, the company had few means of defence against any predator during this period. As one of the Tokyo traders says: 'All you needed was one mutant cell. It was the perfect environment for cancer to grow rapidly and it grew into a tumour beyond all proportions. Before we knew it, it had killed the whole body.'

Until March 1995, Barings plc was chaired by Peter Baring, aged sixty, the exact namesake of the first recorded Baring and the great-great-great grandson of the founder of the bank. Baring had been groomed to run the bank and had always taken a particular interest in the bank's long and glorious history. He joined after Cambridge, when he was twenty-four and the bank was still a modest operation concentrating on trade finance. He had become Chairman in 1989 in succession to Sir John Baring, a distant cousin.

Peter Baring was an unassuming, uncomplicated man with a relatively unostentatious London lifestyle; despite being Chairman he travelled to work by tube, a habit which caused him particular harassment after the bank's crash when he was mobbed by paparazzi. He had always avoided the press, perhaps learning his discretion from his mother, Lady Rose, a former lady-in-waiting to the Queen, whose disdain for 'loose-talk' was typical of the courtiers of her era. His patrician restraint and the immense personal importance of the bank to him was captured in a remark he once made to a reporter: 'I have been with Barings all my working life; that is all you need to know.'

In the eyes of the outside world Baring was in charge, but, as Chairman, he was relatively removed from the day-to-day decision-making process. A comparison might be made with his ancestor Thomas Baring, who, having become distanced from the firm's direction, complained in 1870: 'I do not altogether like when I have been put on top of the tree, to be regarded as a dead branch.' Nonetheless, Peter Baring's aristocratic manner – perhaps not surprising in one with an earldom and four baronies to his name – was clearly remarked by employees and even top management; an employee in Singapore remembers Baring's tour of the office as being 'like a visit from the Queen', an image which stands in marked contrast to Heath's chatty visits.

Although Peter Baring sat at the head of the boardroom table, the man who wielded the greatest executive power was Andrew Tuckey, Barings' Deputy Chairman. His firepower was evidenced by the four muskets which embellished the wall of his eighteenth-floor Bishopsgate office – mementos from the Gordon riots of 1780 when the Bank of England, fearing the worst from a violent mob, distributed firearms to Barings' partners. His office contrasts with those of Heath and Norris. In the early days, Heath had a broom cupboard for an office as he spent most of his time on the trading floor where he had his own desk. However, through the late Eighties all of the senior directors gave themselves massive offices with such expensive furniture that employees used to joke about the £10,000 Italian walnut-topped desks. When Norris arrived he commented on the amount of space taken up by these offices and opted to share one – a goldfish bowl with two glass walls – with Richard Greer and Alex Murray.

In contrast to Baring, Tuckey, fifty-two, was a City outsider. He was born and schooled in Southern Rhodesia, qualified as a Chartered Accountant in the City and afterwards joined British American Tobacco. Two years later, in 1968, he joined what was then called the Company Finance Department of Barings when the division was still very small – only seven or eight people. He became a director in 1973. Tuckey is described by a banking colleague as being 'an extremely capable corporate financier. Very entertaining and very able.' He was largely responsible for revamping Baring Brothers' corporate finance division in the Eighties. Tuckey had a passion for opera and was director of the Royal Opera House and a treasurer of the Friends of Covent Garden.

The executive decisions taken by Tuckey on behalf of Baring Securities were from 1993 based on the strategies drawn up by his protegé Peter Norris, the man Tuckey had implanted as Chief Operating Officer of Baring Securities at the end of the previous year as successor to Christopher Heath.

Both Heath and Norris were charmers of sorts, but while Heath was once described by a friend as 'round and jolly and loveable . . . terribly nice but never struck anyone as an intellectual', Norris's image was somewhat livelier. Having moved into a house on Hong Kong's Victoria Peak with an in-built disco, two-tier pagoda and swimming pool, Norris quickly gained a reputation as a playboy, an image which the *Asian Wall Street Journal* highlighted in a personal profile. In fact, he is a committed family man, but his dapper looks and physical fitness did win him many female fans within the Brothers. 'We had a fan club for him in Barings. All the secretaries were in love with him. They used to send him Valentines,' recalls a female Barings Hong Kong employee.

Norris had joined Baring Brothers as a graduate trainee in September 1976, having gained a first in history and modern languages at Magdalen College, Oxford. He was ear-marked for the corporate finance department and quickly proved to be a rising star within the firm. Stories of his early success reached such mythical proportions that a former Baring Securities branch manager told me that Norris had invented the *Bulldog*, a sterling-denominated Eurobond, in his early twenties. A friend of Norris's put the record straight shortly afterwards when he commented that the individual who accredited him with this 'wouldn't know a Bulldog if one bit him in the leg'. In spring 1984 he left the Brothers for the somewhat racier Goldman Sachs, the US investment bank. At Goldman's, despite his obvious ambition, he was known as an 'all-round good guy'. He worked in the merger & acquisition and corporate finance departments, then moved on to set up the firm's real estate division in London.

In the summer of 1987, Norris was persuaded by Andrew Tuckey to rejoin Baring Brothers as a director and took up the leadership of Baring Brothers' Hong Kong operation, where he was instrumental in the 1988 Hong Kong Telecom flotation. On his return to London in early 1992, Norris and Tuckey worked closely together and were perceived to have such an affinity that they were described to me by a member of Heath's old guard who clearly feels an antipathy towards them, as being as close as 'lips and teeth', a Chinese expression. In his new capacities as Chief Operating Officer and then Chief Executive, Norris increasingly took over the strategic decisions on behalf of the company. 'Peter was driving the business. Tuckey is not a manager, he's a corporate financier,' a bank executive told me. 'Strategy implementation and management structure came down to Peter. Andrew would debate it and Peter implement it.'

In Hong Kong he is remembered as having a strong interest in *fung shui*, the Chinese geomancy system which maintains harmony and good fortune in a dwelling according to ancient spiritual principles of yin and yang; Norris reputedly had a fung shui expert visit his Hong Kong home to drive away the evil spirits and on 8 August 1988 (such an auspicious date for the Chinese that a record number of babies were induced in Hong Kong on that day) he gave HK$88 to every employee in Baring Brothers. Cosmologically, however, Norris's star did not seem to shine so brightly. Not only did the full horror of the Barings collapse come to light on his fortieth birthday (unlucky for the Cantonese), but his personal finances had their hiccups too. Norris was the chief proprietor of the aptly named Duff & Trotter, supplier of vegetables and other comestibles to the gentry, which began life as an off-the-shelf company with the even more apt name of Heave-To, the nautical term for bringing a sailboat to a dead-stop. Duff & Trotter's turnover was good during the Eighties, peaking at £1.44 million in 1988, when City bankers could afford to fork out for Ascot hampers, but profits were more elusive: in that same year it lost £35,000 before tax. Shortly after Norris went to Hong Kong, the firm was rumoured to be in financial difficulties because he was no longer there to manage it personally. 'For all his genius, Norris kept getting hit,' explains an old colleague, 'perhaps because he always focused on his employer's business.'

Such a personal financial disappointment comes as rather a surprise in one who was remarked for his care and caution in business matters. An old friend tells of how Norris, who, like Heath, enjoyed a flutter on the horses, persuaded him to bet £20 on a horse called Artifice during their early days at Baring Brothers, when £20 out of a salary of around £3,000 a year was a sizeable sum. The horse came in last, but when the friend approached Norris to complain, he replied: 'Don't worry. I walked around the whole course before the race. The ground conditions weren't right, so I didn't put the bet on.'

Norris was outstandingly bright and a gifted figures man. 'He is an incredibly capable person who can hold more balls in the air than anyone else I know. He has a mind like blotting paper for detail and is also a man of great personal integrity,' says a colleague in the bank. However, many claim that his intelligence went hand in hand with arrogance and personal ambition, characteristics which earnt him the soubriquet 'Blue Peter' amongst the Management Committee of Baring Securities, a member of which explains: 'because there was no oxygen where his head was'.

There was a widespread perception that Norris harboured a disdain for the broking business which was perpetuated within Baring Securities due to the fact that, although he was not a poor communicator or lacking in understanding, he was not given to superficial charm. Employees within Securities found this difficult to deal with after the fireside-chat manner of Christopher Heath and particularly in light of the fact that they felt personally vulnerable after the turmoil of 1992–3. Norris, as a consummate professional communicated on a direct, strictly business level, and his reluctance to waste time charming people was taken by some to be a sign that he lacked understanding of, or was contemptuous of the Securities arm of the firm. Although Norris was steering the company into a more promising future, many employees hankered for a little reassurance and cajoling after so much turbulence. A long-standing member of the London settlements department recalls an in-house introductory lunch organized for half a dozen Securities' staff from different departments shortly after Norris's arrival. 'He came in and said, "Is everyone here? Who's going to begin?" Various people began to ask questions about the business and he had all the answers and figures at the tip of his fingers, but throughout the lunch no names were mentioned and there were no introductions. How about injecting some enthusiasm into the staff?' Others at grass-roots level cite the fact that neither Norris or Tuckey took their jackets off when they walked about the dealing room. Even Andrew Fraser was reportedly overheard complaining: 'You want our business, you want our profits, come and talk to us. Take your jacket off, walk around the dealing room and talk to people.'

However, although Norris and the troop of bankers he had brought in from the Brothers faced considerable personal and cul-tural resistance from a number of the old-style brokers in Securities, many in the derivatives group, the culture of which did not sit so easily in the firm, welcomed Norris because it seemed that at last someone in senior management understood what they were doing. Norris paid them a high degree of personal attention which, for all that it may have been driven by the group's profitability, was interpreted by some as a genuine interest and understanding of their business.

Employees had ultimately become disillusioned under Heath because they felt that the senior managers who ruled over them did not understand the changes the business was undergoing. A former Securities executive from the derivatives department in Tokyo explains: 'Heath would sit down and spend time talking with you and being charming and you thought he'd understood, but nothing was ever done. Eventually so many people berated him for this that he went round with a briefcase full of A4 pads and pens. He took notes in every meeting, but it was like watching a child take notes.' This may be a little unjust, because Heath did endeavour to address staff concerns, but Norris's response was far more efficient. This perception was enhanced by the completely different image that he cast. The same executive continues: 'In came this athletic, tennis-playing corporate financier with a sharp ear, but more importantly a sharp tongue because he'd listen to what you said and pick holes in it, something Heath never did.'

When Norris stepped in to take charge at Baring Securities, he undoubtedly had high ambitions for the firm. It was Baring, Tuckey and Norris's view (a view furthered on Norris's part, no doubt, by the time he spent at Goldman Sachs), that the future for Barings plc, and the only way of maximizing its capability, was to integrate the disparate parts of the group into an investment bank structure, capitalizing on a closer relationship between the corporate finance and trading operations. By 1995 all parts of the organization were to share the same balance sheet and Brothers and Securities were to be housed under the same roof in new offices at London Wall. The new Baring Investment Bank was to combine the self-discipline of the banking culture with the freewheeling entrepreneurialism of the securities arm.

Baring and Tuckey were concerned about combining the vastly different cultures of Brothers and Securities, but felt that it was the only way forward. Tuckey told the Bank of England: 'I knew that their [Securities] culture was different, as indeed brokers are generally different from corporate financiers anywhere you find them in any organization. I saw that difference . . . in timescale. Everything in the broker's world is today and tomorrow . . . whereas when you talk to a corporate finance person he is interested in what his clients are going to be doing next year. It was the reason why we felt it was right to allow this process of combination to take place over a long period.' Peter Baring agreed on this cultural difference, but said when the plans were announced 'the bank will work more closely with the Securities side. The cultures are different, but they are moving in each other's direction.'

Under Norris's guidance, the emphasis was on long-term strategy, streamlining costs and diversifying and strengthening the existing businesses. This included improving control of financial and risk accounting, better reporting of the firm's overall strategy and status at all levels within the company, and more professional management. Increased management authority was to be delegated to four regional centres (Tokyo, Hong Kong, Singapore and New York), and stronger systems of management control imposed throughout the whole business. To this end, in late 1992 and early 1993, and also in the formation of Baring Investment Bank from May to November 1994, a matrix reporting structure was introduced whereby profit responsibility was on a product basis but with local office management playing an important part in holding together the office infrastructure. This was considered vital because of the strong personalities of key personnel and the desire to co-ordinate product activities on a global basis along with decentralized authority.

Although the new emphasis was to be on streamlining the business, growth had been addictive for Baring Securities and despite the cutbacks of 1992/93 an impressive global network of offices remained, many of them research centres that had no direct revenues attached. Norris focused attention on leveraging the Securities' research and distribution franchise to the full in order to pay for the infrastructural changes and hiring of new management that he planned. His key to growth was broadening the scope of business throughout emerging markets, by leading into new markets and introducing new financial products to the existing emerging market base, in which the broking operation and the rest of the group could work more closely together. To this end the development of Ron Baker's emerging market fixed-income business and the widening of the derivatives business under his control were key.

It was an ambitious plan and one which Norris felt should be implemented as quickly as possible, but in this lay an inherent contradiction. While Norris's plans were long term and well thought-out strategically, he attempted to implement them in the short term. He was personally ambitious and impatient, but, more significantly, employees in Baring Securities, who were restless after the changes, as well as those in Brothers, expected his grand vision to be implemented immediately.

There were considerable dangers inherent in the speed of implementation; the support systems – accountancy, treasury and risk – that Norris inherited, were outdated for the existing business, let alone his planned expansion. There was an enormous push to bring these systems up to scratch, but at the same time, the pace of business developments at least matched that of system improvements. In some new businesses, most notably Ron Baker's Financial Products Group, the front office was way ahead of all the necessary control functions. In addition, existing management found it difficult to cope with the pace of change, and a series of personnel changes following the Turbulence exacerbated the problem.

Norris had not left himself much room for manoeuvre, especially in an environment where he faced personal, professional and cultural resistance to his restructuring programme. 'He genuinely had a vision, genuinely felt that he could leverage off the firm's position in the market to improve the business and turn it into a successful and profitable business, but he couldn't afford for anything to go wrong,' says one of the Baring Brothers' executives in Hong Kong.

Norris made considerable inroads to achieving his aims throughout 1993 and 1994. By the end of 1993 he had successfully lowered operating costs by about £25 million, or 17 per cent. During the second half of 1993, the process of bringing the Brothers and Securities closer together began with the establishment of the new umbrella organization later called Baring Investment Bank. BIB had four groups, of which the most significant were Equity Broking and Trading Group, headed by Norris, and the Bank Group, headed by George Maclean. An important symbolic and practical step towards the combination of the two businesses was the formation of Baring Investment Bank Management Committee in May 1994, chaired by Tuckey (the first committee made up of executives from both Brothers and Securities).

Despite these progressive steps, financial controls and accounts were still in turmoil and risk analysis was poorly understood. Although Heath, Baylis and Martin argue that the control environment was good when they left the firm, with tight cash limits on all the trading books, good risk analysis and complete reconciliation of all transactions, Baring Securities traders tell a different story. They say the accounting system was in chaos when Norris took over, with a lack of uniform methods across different offices: 'We were way back in the Stone Age. The accounts produced in London never matched our figures. They switched accounting methods every time the management changed. We had to rely on guesstimates for most of our costs. It was a farce. You could have hidden anything in those books, absolutely anything,' says one trader.

As the first step towards integrating accounting, risk and treasury departments across the group, Norris enlisted the help of personnel from Brothers to bring Securities' functions into line with the rest of the company. Geoffrey Broadhurst, who had already been brought in from the bank as Securities' Finance Director by Ian Martin, took charge of the accounting problems, while Tony Hawes took charge of Treasury. For risk control, Norris brought in Sajeed Sacranie, who, with substantial help from Richard Johnston, established the basis of a risk-monitoring system. Their efforts culminated in the uniting of risk and funding operations in a new unit called Group Treasury and Risk which became fully operational from August 1994. Ian Hopkins was appointed to the new position of Director of Group Treasury and Risk while Tony Hawes became Group Treasurer.

The senior representatives of each of these new groups, and those of the trading operations that they patrolled, were brought together on a new committee that sat daily to review risk, trading limits and capital funding. The Asset and Liability Committee (ALCO), which superseded the Brothers' Treasury Committee and Securities' Risk Committee, was chaired by Norris and consisted of seven other members: Geoffrey Broadhurst, Group Finance Director; Ian Hopkins, Head of Group Treasury and Risk; Tony Hawes, Group Treasurer; Ron Baker, Head of Financial Products Group; Richard Katz, Head of Equity Trading; Geoffrey Barnett, Chief Operating Officer, and George Maclean, Head of Bank Group. Among the responsibilities of ALCO was to review, assess and monitor credit and market risks across the whole of Barings Group on an ongoing basis. However, it was the responsibility of each product group to manage the risks arising from their own group's activities.

In addition to the revamping of the basic support functions of the company, Norris initiated full reporting of the company's financial and strategic status to the firm's employees. Quarterly board meetings, two in London, one in Asia and one in New York, were initiated at which results were presented in detail, and employees were regularly updated on the financial standing of the company. In response to the changes, Diarmaid Kelly said: 'Peter Norris did an enormous amount of work in cleaning up the operations side, bringing in proper reporting, for instance, and also preparing management accounts which, on occasion, even I could understand. He did it very clearly. He also managed to bring a structure to the firm which had been lacking before. Prior to that, we worked for Christopher Heath and that was about as complicated as management got.'

The task Norris had set himself was mammoth and, given the short time-scale which he had set himself, high-risk. As one banking executive said to me: 'If you look at what he was trying to achieve in 1994, everything was on track, but what he was trying to achieve was very high risk. Administrative anomalies had to be tidied up, management committees had to be set up, more professional people hired. Norris was setting up all kinds of new groups which in themselves were very sensible, but at the same time there was the heavy load of existing business to be seen to and clients to service, as well as the rapid expansion into new businesses.'

While Norris was making every effort to bring support systems up to date, he still had to firefight old problems, particularly in areas where new businesses were developing at a faster pace than the implementation of control systems. In a memo to Peter Norris dated 25 November 1994, Ian Hopkins wrote: 'It is becoming very clear that our systems and control culture are distinctly flaky.' The effort to improve and integrate risk coincided with the ambitious push into proprietary trading by Ron Baker and the Financial Products Group. It was Baker's job to build the business, but he was frequently held back by the lack of these support functions, and members of his team frequently found themselves having to teach back-office staff about the systems needed.

Although staff within the FPG agreed in principle with the bank's plan to expand the proprietary operations which appeared to be fuelling the development of the rest of the business, they argued that the business expanded too quickly before the appropriate risk controls and support networks were in place. 'He [Baker] was pushing too hard. It was grow, grow, grow and spend, spend, spend whereas we should have built on what we had, consolidated and improved it, and then moved ahead,' says a Tokyo trader. 'It was growing faster than the organization could handle. Norris was trying to bring the back office up to speed with the front office, but then Baker came and took the front office further away.'

The regional Asian offices, at a remove from London, continued to cause particular problems. The Tokyo arbitrage team repeatedly asked London for reconciliations on the books to be done earlier, arguing that positions should be matched with the exchange before staff went home each evening, rather than the existing situation whereby the company did not reconcile trades on its books for up to sixteen hours. In addition, because of the different accounting methods used, major discrepancies continued between the figures produced by the traders in Tokyo and the accounts department in London. 'We knew the risk systems were not perfect, but we could only make such a case for it in Tokyo,' continues the same trader. 'We compensated for the lack of risk system by being more self-disciplined. As a result, we were trusted more and it was felt that there was not so much need to speed up the process.'

While Norris was a powerful presence within the reorganized firm, and despite the new emphasis on decentralization and delegation, he was not able to delegate as much as he might have liked. He was unable to hire new managers quickly enough to fill key roles and could not afford to delegate responsibility to some of the existing managers, many of whom remained weak and were unwilling to take decisions without referring to him. 'Management structure in London was not capable of managing the process of integration,' says an executive from the bank. 'Strategy implementation and management structure came down to Norris. He was the only person in the bank with the universal respect of the business as a whole. Peter had people ringing him up with management issues constantly – there was no point in ringing anyone else.'

For instance, the interest Norris showed in their business encouraged the young derivatives traders in Asia in particular to feel that he was approachable, and many took to calling Norris directly. 'A lot of young guys were made to feel very important in the company, as if they had a direct line to God. Of course you don't want a middle man. Strong as Baker was, some of the traders used to call Norris directly on a regular basis,' continues the same Securities executive. 'Norris may have acted above it a lot of the time, but I think he got a kick out of talking to the floor and the traders as if that was where the real action was.'

While the restructuring and the introduction of matrix management in 1993 were intended to clarify the chains of command, the new reporting lines and responsibilities were not perceived to be clear by many, nor were they fully understood. It appears that no complete organizational chart of Baring Investment Bank was prepared and disseminated when the organizational structure was being formulated. To many who had not been used to a strict hierarchy anyway, this probably did not seem much of a concern. Ian Hopkins has said, 'I think, generally, Barings has tended to be unstructured about reporting lines in any case over the years.' However, one of the consequences of this ambiguity was that some members of the management believed that responsibility for certain activities rested with other managers who were later to deny that they had such responsibility.

This situation was exacerbated in Baring Securities' Asian offices where a series of personnel changes took place following Heath's departure and during the reconstruction that eventually left management dangerously weakened, while employees were left wondering who was in charge of which business areas. In Tokyo the long-standing Branch Manager of Baring Securities, Richard Greer, who had been recalled to London to work with Norris, was replaced by Henry Anstey, who only shortly afterwards made way for William Daniel. Daniel had been Baring Securities' chief representative in Indonesia, moving in 1992 to head Seoul. When he left Seoul he was replaced by Gareth Evans, who had been Branch Manager in Zurich. After Daniel's departure from Jakarta, he was replaced by Anthony Davies, previously head of research in Indonesia. Davies then made way for John Marshall, who was formerly in charge of corporate finance in Tokyo.

Hong Kong lost its pre-eminence in the Asian hierarchy in October 1992 when William Phillips, who had set up the firm's Hong Kong office back in the Eighties and was an old and well-respected Barings hand, joined Salomon Brothers. Phillips had been in charge of the Asian securities operations outside of Japan. Phillips's departure heralded another round of staff changes in Hong Kong; the top job went first to Carl Strutt and then to the present incumbent, Jeremy Palmer, who, in May 1995 was appointed Head of Asian Operations. In the meantime a number of big research names jumped ship.

After Phillips's departure, James Bax, who had headed the Securities unit's Singapore and Malaysian operations, inherited his title. Bax had already won a high degree of autonomy for the firm's Singapore and Malaysian operations. Although Baring Securities, like most other international securities houses, had run its non-Japanese Asian operations from Hong Kong, Bax remained in Singapore. A former colleague remembers Bax as a keen golfer who simply enjoyed the more relaxed expatriate lifestyle of Singapore too much to move to Hong Kong.

The upheavals had a direct impact on the Asian derivatives operation. In addition to research personnel, Baring Securities Hong Kong lost equity warrant traders to the start-up operation New China Hong Kong Securities. Most significantly, Richard Johnston, who had been Baring Securities' head of index arbitrage in Tokyo and one of the key players in terms of risk control, returned to London in August 1992 and by May 1993 had left the firm. His departure opened up a gap in the maturity and experience of the remaining team.

A cornerstone of the effectiveness of the new matrix management structure was the integrity and reliability of internal controls at the local level. While significant progress had been made in implementing matrix management throughout the overseas offices, Singapore remained an exception. Simon Jones in particular was considered difficult to manage within the new structure by Norris, in that he was hostile to people outside Singapore and too stridently independent. Norris in fact wanted to get rid of him in 1993, but could not because Bax relied upon him heavily.

Geoffrey Broadhurst, Group Finance Director, has stated that his relationship with Singapore was 'very, very poor' especially with Jones with whom he was barely on speaking terms. Moreover, the fact that Leeson was permitted to have first-line responsibility for both trading and settlements meant that a crucial ingredient in the matrix organization of local integrity was absent in Baring Futures. Management control in London was therefore ineffective in that the executives believed and relied upon the risk and performance information generated by transactions processed in Baring Futures virtually without independent corroboration.

It was against this background of flux that Leeson had risen swiftly to a senior role in the firm. By 1994 the hefty contribution that the young trader and his counterparts in Tokyo appeared to be making to the firm's bottom line through their burgeoning trading activities had won the young General Manager considerable respect and trust within the firm.

His rise came at a time when Baring Securities' Asian operations were again enjoying a period of immense profitability. Following the losses of 1992 and the debacle between Brothers and Securities, the bull markets in Asia in 1993 revived its fortunes and its autonomous spirit. Profits from the securities side soared in 1993 as the region's bourses (excluding Japan) rose by an average of 104.5 per cent. The power and autonomy of Baring Futures (Singapore) was bolstered by its 1994 paper profits, protecting the office from outside interference. Leeson's 'switching' activities alone were reported to have contributed over $30 million of revenue, well over half of the total reported revenue of £52.9 million for the Structured Products Group. One of the more drily amusing moments in the Bank of England's report came when the question was posed by the investigators: 'Was it not a source of great surprise to you that there was this apparent disjoint where you could print money in this way day after day?' To which Peter Baring replied that he found these earnings 'pleasantly surprising'.

The Financial Products Group, headed by Ron Baker, was crucial to the success of Norris's restructuring plan as the revenue from this business made a huge contribution to the organization's bottom line. At the centre of that operation were the Tokyo arbitrage traders and their SIMEX-based counterpart, Nick Leeson. The Tokyo arbitrage team was dependent on Nick's unfailing ability to cope; he was good-natured, organizationally excellent and uncomplaining, despite long hours worked. Indeed, Fernando Gueler told the Bank of England, 'He was so trusted, he was regarded as almost a miracle worker.' Although management knew that the Singapore operation did not fit into the new matrix structure, during the restructuring process, it seemed to be the one part of the firm which was working perfectly; not only was it turning in gargantuan profits, but Leeson appeared to have set up a model of proficiency and professionalism. In fact, Baker frequently held up Leeson and his outfit as a role model.

To many in the firm such perfectionism seemed too good to be true. Leeson had raised the profits in his section far too dramatically, when others knew that, in that kind of trading, such profits were not to be had so consistently. Windfalls, yes. Good months, yes. But month after month, no. And yet, everyone wanted to believe that the profits were real. George Maclean has said, 'Yes . . . people talked about it almost incessantly . . . I have to say that a load of people – all of us, really found it very puzzling. But I have to say, equally, and maybe also naively, we accepted it.' Ron Baker who agrees that he was accountable for the profits of Leeson's switching activities from 1 January 1994, told the Bank of England investigators: 'At that point [early 1994] I never really thought much about why it was so profitable . . . if I had to tell you now what I thought, I thought Nick was a lone star and did his own thing at the time.'

Leeson was on many occasions asked by his colleagues and his bosses exactly *how* he was making so much money. Mike Killian remembers thinking: 'He was making $10 million in one week – doing arbitrage at SIMEX? And Salomons and CRT have got all the computers and years of experience and he's sucking that much out. That sounds like turbo arbitrage to me. How's he doing this? Christ! Let's shut the rest of the place down.'

Mary Walz, Head of Equity Derivatives, and Fernando Gueler had both questioned the scale of Leeson's profits in October 1994, but it was pointed out to them that Leeson had been audited externally and internally. 'How deep can you go? If you go any further you're assuming he's a criminal,' they concluded. Despite the fact that many questions were asked, no one succeeded in eliciting the right answers. The members of ALCO and the Management Committee in London, as well as Leeson's superiors, should indeed have gone deeper.

Leeson's bosses were not the only ones to allow themselves to be fooled. Most staggering of all is the fact that the dangers inherent in Leeson's position as both head of settlements and trading, and the potential for him to abuse it, had been highlighted in an internal audit produced in August 1994. Management in London and Singapore largely failed to heed the warnings and recommendations of this report, though to an extent the auditors made it easy for them to do so.

The 24-page report on Leeson and Baring Futures was conducted over a two-week period in summer 1994 by James Baker. Baker's main sources of evidence were inquiries made of the key managers: the Managing Director, James Bax; Simon Jones, Director; Finance Manager, Rachel Yong, and SIMEX Floor Manager, Eric Chang. The primary source of information was, however, the General Manager, Nick Leeson. While the key reports and records were reviewed, no detailed testing of these records was undertaken.

While the internal audit was part of a routine regional audit carried out for the company, in Baring Futures' case there was a particular emphasis on the staggering profitability of the unit's proprietary trading/arbitrage activities. The report, in its own words, focused on seeking 'answers to some of the questions raised by such exceptional results: Have the rules been broken to make these profits? Have exceptional risks been taken?' In response to these questions, the auditors offered one central criticism: 'The audit found that while the individual controls over BFS's [Baring Futures (Singapore)] system and operations are satisfactory, there is a significant general risk that the controls could be over-ridden by the General Manager [Nick Leeson]. He is the key manager in the front and the back office and can thus initiate transactions on the Group's behalf and then ensure that they are settled and recorded according to his own instructions.' The auditors warned that this was potentially dangerous; Baring Futures was breaking the industry-wide golden rule that a firewall must be established between the front and back offices to ensure that the paperwork corresponds with the deals. Any person with responsibility for both making trades and settling them, most especially if they are the head of both operations, has an open invitation to falsify the details of those trades and the accounts related to them.

The audit noted the excessive concentration of powers in the hands of one individual, in what was a relatively small company with straightforward systems, pointing out that companies commonly divide responsibility for initiating, settling and recording transactions among different areas to reduce the possibility of error and fraud. It listed four duties which Leeson should cease: supervision of the back office team; cheque-signing; signing off on the reconciliation activities at SIMEX; and signing off bank reconciliations. Nick Leeson and Simon Jones agreed that Leeson would cease to perform the functions itemized, yet no significant steps were taken to ensure that the recommendations were implemented.

Perhaps management felt that there was no urgency because, although the report highlighted the inconsistencies with accepted banking practice, it found that Leeson's presence in the back office was desirable: 'Given the lack of experienced and senior staff in the back office, we recognize that the General Manager must continue to take an active role in the detailed operations of both the front and back office.'

Nor did senior Barings managers believe that the volume of transactions was sufficient to warrant a separate treasury or compliance manager at Baring Futures. Exposure to market risk in Singapore was monitored from Tokyo and London using information provided by Tokyo derivatives traders, who monitored positions taken by all traders in the region, and house accounts kept on the system. Nick Leeson was responsible for compliance monitoring and dealing with the regulatory authorities, but there was no compliance officer as such. The audit noted that while high-level monitoring was in place, the weakness of the existing arrangements were that there was no one to review day-to-day trading in detail or to subject dealers and traders to independent compliance monitoring and review. In the report, the response of Simon Jones and Ian Hopkins, Director of Group Treasury and Risk, was: 'We have considered making a similar appointment in Singapore, but are not as yet convinced that there is enough work for a full-time treasury and risk manager even if the role incorporated some compliance duties.' Instead, the task was assigned to Gordon Bowser, the Risk Manager in Hong Kong, who was to undertake independent reviews as and when required – though no such review took place prior to the bank's collapse. Management's complacency was reinforced by the auditors' reassurances: 'In practice the General Manager's powers are limited by external constraints such as customer statement reconciliations in London and SIMEX audits.'

The auditors also commented that Baring Futures was making its profits legitimately: 'Baring Futures has an almost unique capacity to arbitrage effectively between SIMEX and Japanese markets; the arbitrage activity in turn generates opportunities to run positions with limited downside risk . . . The success of the derivatives arbitrage business carried on from Singapore has apparently been achieved without the acceptance of high levels of exposure to changes in the Nikkei 225 index or JGB prices.'

The auditors shared management's view that the retention of Leeson's services was a necessity: 'Although there is some strength in depth in the trading team, the loss of his services to a competitor would speed the erosion of Baring Future's profitability greatly.' A section entitled 'Support for the General Manager' reads: 'The General Manager, Nick Leeson, directs Baring Future's trading on a day-to-day basis in both the JGB and Nikkei 225 pits. Without him Baring Futures would lack a trader with the right combination of experience of trading sizeable lots, a detailed appreciation of the trading strategies, familiarity with the local traders' limits and practices, and contacts among traders and officials. The General Manager likes to be involved in the back office and does not regard it as an undue burden.'

The Bank of England's report concluded that if management had followed up on the important control issues raised by the audit, such as segregating Leeson's duties, imposing gross trading limits and appointing an independent risk and compliance officer, Leeson's unauthorized trading would probably have been uncovered.

Yet the auditor's report, by sanctioning Leeson's continued involvement and not phrasing its recommendations as imperatives, left itself open to interpretation, so that management cannot be held entirely to blame. Moreover, they had the added assurance of four audits carried out during the course of Leeson's tenure in Singapore. Even so, they did question him directly about his activities, but any lingering doubts appear to have been allayed by his sustained enthusiasm to continue his afternoon back office work. Colleagues who worked with Leeson have told me that his reasons for continuing were always that he enjoyed it, he was better at it than anyone else and he wanted to make sure that it was done correctly. Other than that, he had nothing to do after 2.15 p.m. when he left the trading floor. The four audits would have satisfied the majority, but for any who continued to harbour suspicions there remained, as one Barings bond trader said after the bank's collapse, a possible course of action: 'All they had to do was offer him more money for less work and, if he still said no, he'd got to be doing something criminal.' But Leeson's bosses were reluctant to upset their star trader by making such a suggestion; as Andrew Fraser commented, 'in so far as one had a feeling about him [it was] "for God's sake don't interfere".'

It would not have been unnatural if Barings' executives had allowed their judgment to be clouded by Leeson's extraordinary profits, which contributed significantly to the bonus kitty. Baring Securities traditionally paid out 50 per cent of profits before tax, after a capital charge, as bonuses to employees and the 1994 bonus pool, which was due to be paid out in February 1995, was over £100 million. The pool was allocated according to the performance of each product group and the individuals within that group. Four of the top Brothers directors were to receive a total of £4.5 million, while Leeson was in line for £450,000, three times his bonus of the previous year. Many were set to benefit from Leeson's outrageous profitability.

Nick Leeson was the Barings' golden boy; one of Heath's children who had grown up with the firm, married within it and had always appeared to be honest and reliable. In turbulent times, when many areas of the company's business were being revamped and overhauled, the senior executives in London needed to be able to rely on the services of such employees. While aware of the fact that the organization of the Singapore operation was not ideal, it seemed like one problem which could wait.

9 | Pit Bull

'He was the Michael Jordan of the trading floor'
MIKE KILLIAN

The cartoon-like, two-dimensional representations of Nick Leeson in the press fall somewhat short of the reality. In the immediate aftermath of the bank's crash, Leeson was portrayed as a quiet, obscure figure in a large organization, but with a hidden agenda – the sort of man against whom no bank could hope to defend itself. A swift reversal followed a few days later. Leeson was physically and financially conspicuous; not the shy back office clerk secretly plotting sabotage of the bank, but a larger-than-life character who lived for the limelight of the trading floor. In later weeks we were treated to a completely different view of Leeson: 'wholesome' was how his mother-in-law summed him up, the quiet son-in-law who liked nothing better than a night in front of the television with a plate of sausage and mash and his wife by his side. This 'ordinary guy' image is undoubtedly the one which holds the greatest truth, but there are truths contained in the other pictures of Leeson, too. To understand how this juxtaposition of seemingly conflicting character traits became the reality, you have to look beyond media reports and try to comprehend the complex nature of the circumstances in which Leeson was involved. The lifestyle which he led and many of the characteristics that he developed during the unfolding of this saga are common to hundreds of thousands of traders and ex-patriate employees worldwide.

Traders are not born, but bred. They span all strata of society and come from a wide variety of educational backgrounds, ranging from those who have joined a bank straight from school to rocket scientists. They do, however, share common qualities, namely youth, hunger, energy and speed of reaction, as well as a healthy dose of boldness and cocksuredness. Traders' faith in themselves is bolstered by their sizeable salaries; in good years they can earn several hundreds of thousands or even millions of pounds in bonuses. Traders tend not to remain in their jobs for long, but this is not because they crash and burn; it is simply because those who are poor at their jobs are quickly fired and those who are good make enough money to get out fast or move on to manage other traders. Whatever their similarities or differences, they all share training in a homogeneous culture.

In a dealing room or on the trading floor of an exchange (which is simply a more intense version of the same), aside from the telephones and the news screens, there is little contact with the outside world. Most of the day is spent behind desks crammed with computer screens, a sentence which is rarely paroled even for lunch. Traders on an exchange floor are even deprived of natural light, unless they manage to escape from their trading warrens into the sunlight for a lunch break. Although many would find it depressing, to those who know and love it this environment breeds excitement, an excitement which intensifies when big news breaks and the markets become hectic.

Traders live and breathe markets and as a result many live a dangerously isolated existence. The intensity of a trader's work and their complete absorption in the markets demands a level of concentration which does not abate after the markets' close. Traders need to unwind after work, but because of their preoccupation with the markets they follow they usually spend their free time drinking with other traders; many outside the business simply find it too boring to have to listen to their arcane market banter. This is a double-edged sword as it means that it makes it difficult for a trader to escape from his business.

The trading culture is dominated by one simple value system: win or be damned. If you make large profits the rewards, both material and psychological, are colossal. Salaries and bonuses rocket into the hundreds of thousands and the trader is looked upon as a demigod both within his or her company and the wider market-place.

This promotes a strong sense of both personal and corporate greed. Traders aspire to big deals; the amount of money a trader has at his fingertips is a measure of his success, and he will often brag about the size of deals just closed, just as he will brag about his bonus.

The opposite, however, is also true. If the trader makes poor profits he will often be humiliated, finding himself the butt of merciless teasing by fellow traders. Steve Dagleish, a former trader with Barclays Bank, relates how 'the pressure applied to young dealers by their seniors is handed down from the past – primeval instincts of survival. Humiliations in the form of so-called "clever" remarks are either taken with defensive amusement or obvious aggression, handed on down to the last junior in the chain.' Worse than such teasing is the knowledge that a trader who loses money is in danger of losing his job, which would deprive him not only of a salary and other benefits but also the status associated with his work and therefore his friends in the market.

While the crux of the Barings collapse boils down to weakness in management control, the dealing room and trading floor are governed by a more powerful form of control: the psychology of fear. As Karen Weaving, a director of the consultancy group RDI, has noted: 'Underlying this [the value system of the dealing room] is a very common but destructive and dysfunctional way of controlling traders' behaviour: fear. Fear of losing one's job and fear of public humiliation.' She notes that such fear leads to the type of defensive behaviour that undermines good risk management: presenting a macho and arrogant image to fool both oneself and other people into believing you are in control; trading under the effects of alcohol or other drugs; blaming external events and failing to learn from mistakes; denying that the position has gone wrong and believing that the position will come right – tomorrow; even hiding potential or actual losses from management. For example, traders often lie about their trading positions, a phenomenon sometimes referred to as 'bottom drawing tickets' whereby, to avoid discovery when positions have gone wrong, traders hide the tickets in a drawer or simply fail to write them up, in the hope that the positions will return to profitability before anyone finds out. Dagleish recalls one young trader at Barclays in the Eighties who tampered with revaluation rates and hid potentially large losses in a sundry expense account. His indiscretions were spotted early by sharp-eyed settlements clerks and he was dismissed, but having blotted his copybook again in New Zealand and then South Africa, he ended up in prison. 'Perhaps we saw the writing on the wall when he informed the chief dealer in London that his father had died – for the third time .. It was a cry for help.'

Fear leads to an inability to act rationally and cut one's position while the losses are still manageable. It can also lead to the foolish, but common, gamble among losing traders of double or quits. Interestingly, fear can stop traders from being as profitable as they might be; cautious and unconfident traders tend not to take large positions when they are right and equally often run losses or get out of profitable positions early. Fear is not confined to bad traders who should not be in the market in the first place. Many successful traders admit to experiencing this fear and the effects of it. Aside from the wilder manifestations of stress, most traders at times experience a feeling of panic and loss of their rational thought processes which hinders them from making good decisions under pressure and can easily result in loss-making situations.

In the run up to the listing of British Telecom in the Eighties, a young trader at a US investment bank in London bought a large number of Cable & Wireless shares, the only listed communications company at that time, from a fund manager who wished to sell. What the trader hadn't realized was that the rest of the market was about to sell Cable & Wireless in favour of British Telecom. Over the next few weeks the price of C & W began to fall, and as he realized his mistake, the trader bought many more of the shares, hoping that by doubling up he would eventually compensate for his losses. But as the day of the listing approached and the price of C & W shares continued to plummet, he grew more and more terrified. Unable to cope with the idea that he had made such a mistake, he took on further C & W shares until he found himself holding $30 million worth of the issue. British Telecom was launched to huge success and the trader was beside himself at the thought of the mammoth losses he had incurred. Luckily the story has a happy ending. The BT issue was oversubscribed and investors flocked back to C & W to retain their exposure to the communications sector. As the price rebounded, the trader was saved.

It is often said that traders playing with figures on a screen or on an exchange floor are like gamblers who, once they have converted their cash into plastic chips, lose all sense of its real value. I would say this is seldom true. Traders are all too conscious of the amounts of money they are making or losing. Such fear is evidenced by frequent trips to the bathroom, by the chain smoking of cigarettes and by the long term damage to their health caused by ulcers, drink and drug problems.

I remember Nick as a friendly, down to earth, almost meek guy, whose loudness when drunk merely seemed to over-compensate for his shyness on other occasions. On visits to the Tokyo office, he was cheerful and helpful. In the evenings he was always ready to go out for drinks and to nightclubs with his colleagues. There was nothing unusual about such evenings; Barings employees always expected to be entertained on overseas trips, just as those who were doing the entertaining rallied to the occasion. It was an excuse for everyone to go out and have a good time and it boosted office camaraderie. Nick was much like any other trader. In his suits and general appearance he looked no different to other English brokers I have known in their late twenties and his drinking capacity was no lesser or greater. His escapades when drunk were certainly not unusual for a trader. Indeed, compared with the renowned flamboyance of some others I know in the business, he was downright ordinary. Most who knew him agree with this view. A former member of the index arbitrage team in Tokyo remembers: 'He was tame in comparison with the guys in Tokyo. By the standards of Barings' party animals he was definitely not in the top league.'

This doesn't necessarily conjure up the image of what is commonly perceived to be a typical trader, nor does it stand up to many of the pictures of Nick which have been painted in the media. But traders are changed by their working environments. It was the culture and atmosphere in which Leeson worked that developed the potential he already had to make him into a respected trader who was ultimately feared in the pit by many of his contemporaries, but in the process certain aspects of his personality were also to change. A derivatives trader in London explains: 'There's a sub-culture in an exchange. Exchanges like LIFFE are 75–80 per cent composed of aggressive young males. They're just kids. If a pretty girl walks on to the floor everyone whistles. If a guy comes in wearing a check shirt everyone starts jeering and shouting "poofter". In a normal environment these guys would be normal, but at work they're affected by the culture. Losing and making money does affect you. You can be shy, but where money's involved it changes you.'

The metamorphosis of Nick Leeson's character was not specific to either himself or the environment created at Barings. It was symptomatic of a certain type of trading culture: one of individual-ism, competition and insecurity, in which greed and fear are para-mount characteristics. Such an environment negates traditional management and risk controls, namely the cultivation of teamwork rather than individual competitiveness, the sharing of information and the nurturing of self-confidence. Arrogance is not self-confidence. The latter helps you to admit when you are wrong and be open with colleagues and bosses. Arrogant traders suffer from an illusion of invulnerability, which is encouraged by less confident colleagues deferring to them, and managers being unwilling or unable to challenge them.

Unsurprisingly, the stress level among traders and, to a lesser extent, sales staff, is high. Each individual reacts differently to stress, but it regularly manifests itself in most traders in outlandish behaviour. I recall watching a salesman, still drunk from the night before, jumping up and down on his desk singing 'Scotland the Brave' at seven in the morning and waving his fist in the air – until he punched a hole in the ceiling and decided that the best course of action was to take himself home to bed. Taking comfort in the bottle was always a favourite form of relaxation for most traders in Tokyo in the Eighties and I'm sure it still is.

Whereas most corporations value circumspection, trading floors foster a more extrovert approach, where even erratic behaviour, such as wearing women's hosiery on their heads and waving bottles of vodka, is tolerated and thus unwittingly encouraged. A strong

by-product of this is emotional volatility, which is frequently over-looked as managers focus on the financial rewards which are being reaped for the firm. And yet, stress-related emotional volatility, combined with over-confidence and large trading positions is a potent recipe for disaster.

Living in a foreign community with such strong financial support as is provided for most ex-patriates in the financial industry naturally engenders a feeling of both isolation and elitism. It is quite common for these circumstances to exacerbate the already over-confident behaviour of many traders.

The packages offered to ex-pats in this industry typically include: a similar base salary to that they would make in their home country plus a cost-of-living adjustment which may reflect an element of perceived social hardship in the posting, and company-financed luxurious accommodation. Additional benefits which may accrue, depending on the individual's company and the country, include a company car, the paying of utility bills and the cost of children's school fees.

The removal of such day-to-day responsibilities as maintaining a home and paying bills, when combined with the loss of maturity, wisdom and emotional support which ensues from the extreme distancing of older family members and long-standing friends, creates a vacuum. It is rare for companies or individual managers to make any attempt to help fill this vacuum. Thus in a working environment that already breeds arrogance, the creation of a vacuum accompanied by a frequently significant increase in personal wealth, engenders among younger, more impressionable employees in particular, a feeling of superiority that can manifest itself in undesirable ways. For instance, one broker I know in Asia insists that his maid calls him 'Master', instead of the customary 'Sir'. Alcohol exacerbates this sense of near invulnerability. To reach the dining area of *Manin*, a Philippe Starck restaurant in Tokyo, diners must descend three sheer flights of shallow granite steps, down which many a drunken customer has fallen. Narrow granite girders stretch from the top of these stairs out across the restaurant. One evening a drunk trader ran out across one of the girders, hovering precariously above the tables some 100 foot below. He remained there until the terrified Japanese manager and several waiters fell to their knees and begged him to come down.

Nick Leeson was no different from many young ex-pat traders. He had worked hard for his opportunity to shine and was rewarded with a posting with increased responsibility in Singapore. Having left London, his family and his £25,000 a year salary behind him, the confidence of this quiet, unassuming guy from Watford grew in leaps and bounds in Asia. By Christmas of the same year he was already making his mark in the Nikkei trading pit on SIMEX.

His day was spent in the hectic environment of the SIMEX floor in the Overseas Union Bank centre at One Raffles Place in the heart of the business district. SIMEX is a small market where everyone knows everyone – and everyone knew Nick Leeson. Sporting the striking navy-and-gold stripes which are Barings' trading colours, he cut an imposing figure even amongst the kaleidoscope of the hexagonal SIMEX pit; standing head and shoulders above his predominantly Asian counterparts, he was noisier and tougher than everyone else and this very physical advantage must have enhanced his feeling of superiority.

Leeson would stand in the pit yelling out orders relayed to him by hand-signal by his colleagues in the Barings booth or phoned to him directly by clients or his colleagues in Barings offices by telephone. From time to time when the market went slack, he would dash back to his booth to write tickets or chat to his colleagues in the Tokyo and Osaka offices. Those colleagues would keep him informed about the minutest market movements on their own computer screens while he in turn would tell them about developments in the market over the squawk box.

After the closing bell at 2.15 p.m., he would gather up his notes, leave SIMEX and stroll across Raffles Place to the Baring Futures office on the 24th floor of Ocean Towers. There his afternoons were spent overseeing the settlement of trades transacted that day and reconciling cash balances and positions with clients, the Exchange, and Barings' Tokyo, Osaka and London offices.

Invariably, once the paperwork was clear, the local bars were the next stop. Here Leeson would unwind with other ex-pat traders on SIMEX; he rarely socialized with locals, preferring to go out with a small group of Western friends and sometimes clients. Harry's Quayside, situated on Boat Quay by a bend in the Singapore river, was a favourite haunt only a five-minute walk away from the office. Five years ago the Singapore river was full of sampans and Boat Quay was lined with hawker stalls. Now it is a smart, tree-lined esplanade which forms a crescent round the river. The shop-houses have been converted into a parade of smart bars and restaurants painted in pastel shades of turquoise, cream, terracotta and apricot which cater for tourists and the local and ex-pat population; the hawker stalls have made way for tables and chairs shaded by large canvas umbrellas for those who want to sit outside in the daytime and watch the world go by. In the evening, diners sit in the glow of candlelight, watching the lights reflected in the water from the buildings opposite.

Harry's is the first bar on the strip as you approach it from the business district, but it is one of the best, being voted Singapore's Night Spot of the Year. The interior is dark with a long wooden bar sporting a Smirnoff fruit tank for vodka shots; there is a small stage in one corner for the jazz bands which perform nightly, and an open tiled area with high round tables and wicker and metal stools around which the crowds sway in the evenings. A brass placard on the wall sets out the house standards:

This bar is dedicated to
those splendid fellows who
make drinking a pleasure
reach contentment before capacity
and who, whatever they drink
can take it, hold it, enjoy it
and still remain gentlemen.

On warm weekday evenings, jazz notes spill out on to the stone walkway outside which is swollen with crowds of bankers and brokers swilling glasses or jugs of Heineken and the local beers, Anchor and Tiger. The music is almost drowned out by the noise of the boys reliving the trades and tales of their day or talking loudly into their mobile phones, though the atmosphere remains relaxed and parochial. 'This is heaven. Tell me your definition of heaven. For me, this is it,' Leeson once said to a friend.

The Malaysian bartender, who has been at Harry's for years, knows Leeson well: 'He came here nearly every night, especially Friday. He was a very friendly guy, very quiet. I never could believe what he did to the bank. I didn't see him for a few days and then I heard about it . . . Harry's has become famous because of Nick Leeson.'

Leeson's ability to please Barings' clients and the firm's traders in Tokyo by his apparently superb execution of their orders soon had a dramatic impact on his own remuneration. Only a year after he had joined the SIMEX floor he was paid a bonus of £130,000 and his salary was increased to £52,000. He was anticipating a bonus of £450,000 in February 1995 which, according to Lisa, was one of their reasons for staying on in Singapore despite the mounting pressure of Nick's job.

But success is a double-edged sword. Although his material rewards and prospects of career advancement were good, the psychological aspects of his performance on SIMEX were no less tangible. People began to view him differently. 'He wasn't exactly turning into a jerk, but he was feeling a hell of a lot more confident than when he was just a futures and options clerk because he was getting a lot of accolades from everyone. Management, the clients loved him,' says Mike Killian. 'It was go Nick, go Nick, go, go, go! His head was spinning. He was the Michael Jordan of the trading floor.' Ron Baker was reportedly so impressed with him that he had spoken to Leeson about going to Hong Kong and Brazil to set up similar operations there. Success was spectacular enough to send Leeson into a stratosphere of self-belief. He became, both in his own eyes and in the eyes of those around him, the king of the trading floor. In 1994 he changed the password for his electronic mail to Superman.

Leeson had always had a good client order flow to execute, but as Barings' business increased and the discretion he had with those orders grew, he gained a dominant position in the market place. The more powerful he became, the more his reputation grew. He was now respected to the point of reverence. Friends and fellow SIMEX traders were now unanimous in their expressions of belief in him, though few of them, no doubt out of embarrassment, are willing to put their names to these comments now: 'It wasn't just that he got it right all the time, but his seeming confidence bordered on arrogance. He didn't just get it right, he appeared to be cock-sure that he was going to get it right.' Other traders used to monitor what Leeson did to pick up tips on how and what types of risk they should be taking. Comments such as 'He had some kind of Midas touch. Everything he touched was gold', or 'You felt that he could make or break the market', are typical. 'Before this happened we thought he was very brilliant, the most confident trader around town. He seemed to be able to move markets,' says another trader. A Barings trader who worked with Leeson for a while on the SIMEX floor told me about the experience. Wanting to give the impression that Barings were the kings of the pit, the trader once said, 'When Nick came on to the floor the other traders used to bleed from their ears', a comment which shortly after the crash invited the response from a colleague: 'and now we're bleeding from our arses'.

It was not just his new-found notoriety at SIMEX, but the squeaky-clean, sun-drenched environment of Singapore and all the trappings of an ex-pat lifestyle that Nick was referring to when he described his new life in Asia as 'heaven'. Singapore is a booming city at the hub of one of the world's fastest growing regions, but that is to suggest that it is large and busy. In fact, in many respects it is quite the opposite; the island is small and parochial and, with its neat, model-like buildings set in lush green surrounds, it offers the perfect suburban life. The streets are free from beggars, litter and chewing gum. The local people are friendly, overwhelmingly polite and relaxed, and the atmosphere safe and comforting. Though rather too sterile for some, to many it is a veritable Paradise.

Although Lisa was homesick, she grew accustomed to the benefits of living in this tropical island state, travelling around the city quite happily by MRT (Mass Rapid Transport) and bus. While Nick worked, she would go to the gym, membership of which came with Nick's job, and potter around with girlfriends during the day – many, like her, wives of Barings employees. Although Lisa had resigned her job before her marriage in 1992, she still felt part of the Barings community and when the Futures' back office was short-staffed after the bonus had been paid in 1993, she volunteered to help out by doing unpaid clerical work for a few months. She also worked occasionally in the local kindergarten.

In such a cosy, cocooned environment where life is quite unreal compared to the harsher reality of the US or UK, it is easy to see how Nick Leeson could have persuaded himself that he couldn't put a foot wrong. Even his transgressions probably did not seem real to him. A friend of mine who was born and brought up in Singapore and now heads a derivatives team in London remembers: 'There is no conception of the violence, poverty and graffiti of the

UK in Asia, especially Singapore. It's Disneyland. If there's no Coke in the fridge you just call up the store and a case will be sent up; you don't have to pay for it or even sign anything. The longer you spend out of a more realistic environment, the more it affects your sense of judgment in terms of deciding what's right or wrong.'

Nick and Lisa moved into a S$5,000 (£2,500) a month three-bedroom apartment paid for by Barings in Angullia View, an apartment block just off the ritzy main-drag Orchard Road at 29 Angullia Park, a leafy boulevard lined with expensive hotels and shops. There are twenty-four apartments in the block, a white building set in neatly manicured grounds in one of Singapore's most fashionable neighbourhoods, where Tamil and Malay workers come in every morning to mow lawns, wash cars and sweep the grounds. Angullia View has round the clock security and an outdoor pool. The Leesons shared the fifth floor with three other families: Taiwanese, Japanese and Singaporean.

Singapore apartments are expensive but not particularly glamorous; while pricey, their new home was only in the mid-range of typical ex-pat housing, but it was still, of course, a veritable palace compared to the homes of most of the local staff. Nor was it particularly lavish inside. The walls were painted off-white and the carpet was cream, as in many rental apartments in Asia. It was furnished with simple, locally produced cushion-covered rattan furniture and a couple of hard wood Asian chests. Nick and Lisa had put up pictures on the walls and large palm plants added a touch of greenery to the living room and the balcony which ran around the apartment. Otherwise the place was relatively bare, with few personal touches bar the wedding photos one would naturally expect from a newly married couple proudly displayed on shelves in the main room. One of the Leeson's neighbours commented to me after their departure: 'They had a good time here. Just look at the place. With all that money, how could they not have had a good time?'

A typical weekend for the Leesons would begin with Friday night out on the town with friends. On Saturday Nick would play golf with his friends at one of Singapore's immaculate golf courses, or soccer – he played for the Barings side and for the Admiralty Club, a local third division league team where he was one of two foreign players in the squad. But his soccer skills were not, according to those who played with him, particularly impressive in comparison with the light-footed, football-mad Malays. On Saturday night they often watched a football match on TV with a few friends, while Sundays were spent visiting the cinema or shopping.

Nick bought his own car, a black Rover. The couple also had access to the company boat, *Baring Up*, and the opportunity to take trips into Malaysia, just a 45-minute drive across the Johore Causeway, and other resorts around the region.

Nick and Lisa planned to stay in Singapore until they had saved enough money to return to the UK; they had used his 1993 bonus to buy a house in the pleasant South London suburb of Blackheath. They intended to start a family in the near future (Lisa had a miscarriage in January 1995).

As would be expected, the Leesons' tastes became more sophisticated during their stay in Singapore as Nick's income increased. Nick remained a regular patron of Harry's, but also began to frequent a row of bars closer to home in the pretty, cobbled Emerald Hill. One of those he particularly enjoyed was 5 Emerald Hill, an establishment patronized by the artistic community. Number 5 is an understated place with peeling paint and drifts of monkey nut shells on the floor. Films are shown regularly upstairs. Cooled by the colonial-style overhead fans, Leeson listened to jazz and soul music and, according to the bartender I spoke to, cultivated a taste for wine. Lisa's tastes also became refined; though she wore sweat pants around the apartment block in the day, she developed a liking for designer clothes. Singapore boasts a large number of smart marble-floored shopping malls full of designer boutiques where staff offer an attentive service. Many of the best were just minutes' walk from her home.

To many of Nick's close friends and colleagues at Barings, he remained the normal bloke, who enjoyed his sausages and mash and pint of lager and the company of his wife and good friends. Most say that both in and out of work he was the same modest guy everyone knew back in England. 'He was pretty quiet most of the time, an unassuming, almost humble guy,' says one of his trading counterparts in Tokyo. 'He'd talk about soccer with me, about where he'd been out the night before. He'd crack jokes and then we'd chat about the market.' Many of those friends and colleagues in Singapore and Tokyo, however, had become acclimatized to the ex-pat lifestyle and may even have taken it for granted. A significant part of this acclimatization involved making light of behavioural excesses and the more unsavoury personality changes which inevitably result from time spent in a cocooned environment.

It was friends and family at home who were most shocked by Leeson's behaviour as reported in the media. They were unwillingly forced to realize that his quiet personality had changed and that there was a side to his character which had previously remained hidden. Around town Leeson increasingly epitomized the worst excesses of an ex-pat trader abroad; although revered by fellow traders, he clashed with the local population and, like many a highly-strung dealer, went on loud and crass drinking sprees with his colleagues and behaved badly.

Leeson was a big fish in a very small pool, both at work and socially. It is easy to see how in such a parochial environment he felt more important and more powerful than everyone else, both fellow ex-pats and locals alike. It is also easy to understand how he could have convinced himself that he could get away with anything he wanted to.

A prime example of the obnoxious behaviour of Leeson and his friends occurred in early October 1993 when Leeson was banned for a year from the Singapore Cricket Club following a racist attack on a club official of Indian extraction. The incident took place around the billiard tables of the men's bar. Leeson was asked, as was customary, to produce his membership card before playing snooker with his two guests. The group had been drinking heavily that evening and Leeson was affronted at not being recognized. He refused to produce his card, and when Anandar Kumar, a member of the billiards committee, intervened to ask Leeson again, he was verbally abused by one of the party, being called a 'fucking black bastard' and other equally outrageous assaults. Despite this, Leeson and his friends were allowed to play a game, but the abuse continued sporadically throughout the evening. Later that night when Kumar departed, he was followed outside by members of Leeson's party who taunted him until a scuffle broke out in which punches were thrown. Kumar could not confirm that Leeson had been one of the men who punched him, but this incident led to a twelve-month suspension of Leeson's club membership for failing to control his guests. Prior to this punishment being imposed, Leeson wrote a letter of apology to Mr Kumar, saying the incident left him 'highly embarrassed'. However, some who knew him in Singapore say that this typified his attitude. He felt that he was riding the wave, he was the master and could get away with anything.

Barings' staff members have told me that such arrogant, obstreperous behaviour was accompanied by what could at times be an almost contemptuous attitude towards money. This is a significant point for a man who daily was risking the bank's capital. Indeed, a former Barings staffer in Tokyo tells me that he thought Leeson had 'a Space-Invader mentality' as far as his trading was concerned. At an off-site seminar weekend held in New York for all 150-plus members of the Financial Products Group globally in December 1994, Leeson, on the way to a holiday with Lisa in a luxury hotel in Ireland (a last respite from what was to prove a gathering maelstrom), was in typically fine form. At around three in the morning on the Saturday night, Leeson, along with fifteen other members of the party, ended up in a bar in downtown New York which served vicious cocktails in foot-long plastic glasses shaped like sharks and whales, sharks being turquoise and whales pink. The whole party was already reeling and had begun to hit each other over the heads with the empty glasses, when Leeson and one other member of the group bet a third party $300 each that he wouldn't down a Vodka Martini composed of at least a quarter-pint of vodka in one. While the guy was considering the prospect, Leeson fell asleep with his head on the bar. He was woken, somewhat confused, several minutes later by congratulatory cheers and guffaws, and was told that he owed the drinker $600. He promptly got out his bulging wallet and placed six one-hundred dollar bills on the bar top as if they were peanuts. The next morning, nursing a sore head over breakfast, he pulled out the same wallet and said: 'God, I must have had a good time last night.'

Leeson was not universally popular with the predominantly

young and female back office staff under his control at Futures. 'It was as if he had a multiple personality. He was nice to his friends and very hospitable to both friends and clients – he'd always be there to pick you up at the hotel and take you out if you were visiting – but he was arrogant on the trading floor and aggressive to the back office staff. He ruled those girls with an iron fist,' says an arbitrage trader in Tokyo. One of Barings' SIMEX floor traders recalls that Nick 'had very little patience, a very short fuse about mistakes. If his subordinates made an error, he would lose his cool.'

Leeson himself was subject to little management control and was to a large degree a law unto himself. While some in Singapore were beginning to view him as a liability due to his obstreperousness, especially when drunk, the Barings management still billed him as an ever-brightening star. So long as Nick continued to print money for the company, they seemed prepared to overlook behaviour which might have been censured in a more junior employee who made a less direct contribution to the firm's bottom line. Thus Nick's success earned him considerable licence.

It was Leeson's 'bottom line' which led Barings' senior management to take an active role in suppressing a particularly embarrassing story with regard to his outlandish behaviour. In October 1994 Leeson, the market's darling, was riding particularly high. He had just collected, on behalf of Barings, a prize from SIMEX for attracting the highest individual amount for customer volume trading, presented at a lavish dinner in the presence of Lee Kuan Yeu, Singapore's former Prime Minister. In celebration of this success, Leeson went on his customary round of bars with a bunch of trading friends and ended up in a restaurant where, in a display of high spirits, he dropped his pants at the table. Singaporeans are not renowned for their sense of humour and his fellow diners and the restaurateur did not share Leeson's colleagues' amusement at being presented with a pair of buttocks while they slurped their noodles. The police were called and – unsurprisingly in a nation which throws people behind bars for chewing gum or dropping litter – Leeson woke the next morning with a throbbing hangover to find himself in the slammer.

Local feeling about foreigners' bad behaviour was running particularly high at that time in the wake of the much-publicized public flogging of an American youth who had been caught vandalizing cars. The youngster had been made a prime example of the nation's intolerance for such behaviour, despite a protest from the US government emphasizing the inhumane manner of the punishment. In the sober light of day, Leeson and his bosses were quick to realize that the same pair of buttocks which had been displayed in the restaurant risked further public exposure.

Leeson was later to boast that Barings executives had come to his assistance, quickly extracting him from jail. Had they not intervened, Leeson faced a humiliating punishment, or even expulsion from the country, which would have resulted in embarrassing publicity for SIMEX, given that Leeson had been held up as a role model by the exchange.

Barings took further steps to prevail upon *The International Financing Review*, which had caught wind of Leeson's antics from traders on the SIMEX floor, not to write it up in their gossip column, *L'Eminence Noire*. Leeson's fame had already led to a profile in the Asian edition of *Futures and Options World*, accompanied by a photo of him in his trading jacket, which has since made that particular freelance photographer a fortune.

In a bid to save Leeson's bacon, as well as their own, Barings requested that the magazine drop the piece. In a display of gentlemanly spirits, the editors agreed to tone it down to a level where only those in the know would understand.

More remarkable still was the fact that, despite the trouble caused, according to Leeson himself, there was no official rebuke from his seniors at Barings. The tale became one of his favourite after-dinner stories, just as the original incident – which took on many different guises in the press during the months following the bank's collapse – has now become apocryphal. I was told of this escapade myself at a dinner in Hong Kong just a month or so before the bank's demise.

The *International Financing Review* was understandably very quick in the wake of the collapse to point out in its March 1995 edition that, had Barings not pleaded for the story to be dropped, the firm

might not have found themselves in the nasty predicament that
followed shortly after.

> We have a tragic footnote to the collapse of the Barings dyn-
> asty. Without wanting to sound too self-important, the whole
> thing might have been avoided had we published last autumn
> a hair-raising tale on the antics of Mr Leeson ... Would
> Barings still be around if we had run the story? Would Leeson
> have been expelled from Singapore with his tail between his
> legs, and sent off to run derivatives in Mexico? And would his
> fatal trades thus have never happened? We have a horrible
> feeling that the answer to all three questions is 'yes'.

The press have been quick to draw comparisons between Leeson
and other notorious rogue traders of recent years. While the characters, backgrounds and circumstances of these rogues vary, they
share one outstanding point of similarity, namely the culture in
which they were nurtured. The trading culture breeds personal and
corporate greed, a strange mélange of over-confidence and fear, not
to mention hubris. In Leeson's case, this attitude was exacerbated by
a feeling of superiority engendered by his cosy, Singaporean ex-pat
lifestyle.

There are some who put Leeson into the category of the poorly
trained guard dog. A member of the futures and options broking
department sums this view up as follows: 'If you train a puppy to
be an attack dog and it gets off its leash and kills someone, do you
blame the dog for doing what it was taught to, or do you blame
the trainer for not leashing the dog properly?'

It is certainly true that Leeson's bosses made it easy for him to
slip off the leash and there are many lessons to be learnt from this.
The lust for profits within Barings was no greater than that in any
other securities firm, but the atmosphere and attitude within the
firm was perhaps significantly more opportunistic than most and
the management controls were lax. It was senior management that
dictated Leeson's trading limits, his reporting lines, it was they who
allowed him control of both the trading and settlements departments and who were responsible for the environment in which he
worked.

However, to suggest that lax controls alone are to blame for what happened is to miss part of the point. It was not only the absence of external controls which were at fault, but the fact that Leeson lacked the internal controls which keep others in check. There are hundreds of Leesons in dealing rooms and trading floors across the globe, but not all of them get off the leash, nor do they want to. Despite being in an environment which blatantly encourages greed for both corporate and personal remuneration and which to many outside the industry would seem to offer daily temptation to err from the straight and narrow, most traders retain their integrity. They simply do their job – to make as much money as is humanly possible, legally – to the best of their ability and retain a healthy set of personal scruples. It would be doing the vast majority a disservice to suggest otherwise.

So what happened to Nick Leeson? I believe that his desire to please – his clients, fellow traders and managers – and his fear of displeasing them, was so great that he went to absurd lengths to achieve what he wanted. His desire, and proven ability, to please others may in turn have led to the realization that he could also please himself. In the sunny, unreal cocoon of Singapore where he was King of the local exchange, it was easy for him to convince himself that he was doing nothing wrong and, just as there were very few around who challenged him, there was almost no one in that puritanical city who imagined that he had indeed left the straight and narrow.

10 | Error Account 88888

'Apologies, Nick'

Nick Leeson's job on the trading floor required a specific set of skills including speed and decisiveness, but was, by financial market standards, relatively simple. Or it ought to have been. This view was expressed in no uncertain terms by Ron Baker who, to Leeson's visible irritation, was overheard saying that a monkey could do it.

When down on the exchange, Leeson executed orders for clients, sometimes speaking to them directly from the trading floor, but more often having orders relayed to him by colleagues in the office. As Barings had the largest flow of client orders in the market, Leeson already had enough firepower in the pit to be considered a major gunslinger. In addition, he would execute orders on behalf of the index arbitrage team in Tokyo that were relayed to him by squawk box, an open line. The proficiency with which he executed these orders appeared to improve rapidly and so he was given increasing discretion with these transactions, until the overall scale of business he had to execute enabled him to exert significant influence on the market.

Eventually his remit from the Tokyo arbitrage team was expanded to allow him full discretion to exploit the frequent but minute price differentials between the futures contracts traded on SIMEX and similar contracts traded on the Japanese exchanges. As the Japanese exchanges were screen-based and SIMEX was open outcry, office staff in Osaka and Tokyo would keep Leeson and his booth staff in constant touch with every change in the price registered on their screens, so that he could trade in the pit and immediately advise them to match it with an opposite trade in Japan or vice versa. Price anomalies might last only seconds, so speed was of the essence. This 'switching' activity was supposed to be almost risk-free as every purchase on one exchange was intended to be offset within seconds by an equal sale on the other, although occasionally if the market moved in his favour on one of the positions, Leeson would let it run for a while, an action known as 'lifting a leg' or 'legging in and out' of trades. At the end of the day, all positions were supposed to be netted out so that the long and short positions were equally matched. The profitability of these trades could be quite significant, but only when executed in large volume. But that was not all Leeson was doing.

Leeson went off the rails almost as soon as he arrived in Singapore in the spring of 1992. It is now evident that all of his apparently profitable business was in fact bogus. Leeson had built up a hidden cumulative loss of £2 million by the end of 1992, which grew to £23 million by the end of 1993, £116 million by June 1994 and £208 million by December of the same year. At that point his losses were slightly greater than the profit of £205 million made by the group as a whole before accounting for tax and £102 million of bonuses. On 27 February 1995, Leeson's losses had ballooned to the fantastical figure of £827 million. As a SIMEX floor trader put it shortly after the bank's crash: 'He lied about everything; none of his profits were real.'

Leeson's dodgy trading was booked through Account 88888, a number chosen for its lucky auspices in Chinese numerology. The account was set up in July 1992 by a software technician who established Baring Futures operational systems; it was designated internally as a 'client' account and described as an error account on the firm's system. Error accounts are a common phenomena in futures trading operations. In broking businesses like that which Leeson ran, if a trade is miscommunicated, incorrectly executed, or for any other reason is not agreed to by a client, then it is booked into an error account. Error positions such as these are almost always closed out immediately and the resulting profit or loss included in the overall figures of the broking operation. Naturally one would not expect active trading to take place in these accounts, nor large profits or losses to accrue.

At its inception, Account 88888 was included in the daily trading reports sent electronically to London. But on 8 July 1992, Dr

Edmund Wong, a systems consultant to Baring Futures, received specific instructions from Nick Leeson to change the software programme to exclude Account 88888 from all these reports, with one exception: the margin file. It therefore appears that Leeson intended to use 88888 for unauthorized activities from the outset, deliberately excluding it from Barings' files and records.

In London, Barings' management and other personnel were apparently not aware of the existence of this account until 23 February 1995. Although the daily margin file explicitly included the balance on 88888, since no such account number existed in the master file the balance was left in a suspense file. There were no procedures or controls in place to review, analyse or evaluate items in this suspense file.

In Singapore, the back office staff and a number of the floor trading team were fully aware of the existence of Account 88888, as they were writing tickets, booking trades and adjustments those trades on a regular basis from the day the account was opened. However, despite the increasingly unusual nature of some of the transactions, they appear to have been unaware of the extent of the account's abuse and did not think to question it with management. Leeson was in total control of the back office, had hired and trained most of the young and largely female staff himself, as he had the floor personnel. His scope for circumventing the accounting system and avoiding traditional audit trails had been pointed out in early 1994 by Tony Hawes and highlighted in the internal audit of August 1994. Leeson had indeed been flagrantly abusing his position and actively trading through 88888 since 1992.

Leeson's experience in London and Jakarta had given him an intimate understanding of the settlements process. This knowledge, in conjunction with his command of the back office, enabled him to easily pull the wool over the eyes of his superiors, internal and even external auditors. He was in a position where no one could challenge him without seriously questioning his fundamental integrity, a confrontation which he successfully gambled would never occur. The account records that were printed daily for all internal and client trades were retained in the settlement archives and the second copies sent to clients. For the misused Account 88888,

Leeson left standing instructions with his settlement staff to shred the bottom copy and give him the top copy, so the only record of his trades in the whole company was in his hands. 'The girls in the back office were naive really,' comments a member of the settlements department in Hong Kong. 'Everyone really rated Nick and did what he said. Even if they had known something was wrong they would have been too scared to say it. That's office politics.' Mike Killian confirms this view: 'They're young girls. They were just doing what the boss said. He was top dog, a guy that used to go out to dinner with the Chairman of SIMEX. They were unwittingly involved because they trusted him.' In October 1994 the group treasurer Tony Hawes met one of these clerks on a visit to Singapore and, according to an internal memo, 'gained a very unfavourable impression of her understanding of futures and options'. She was 'quite unable to explain a single entry of $100 million'. An 'unsatisfactory discussion' ensued in London between Leeson and Hawes about this entry.

The core of Leeson's unauthorized trading activities which sparked the fire that ultimately engulfed the bank was Nikkei 225 options trading. From the end of 1992, Leeson sold put and call options on the Nikkei 225 index, a strategy to which he consistently adhered up to the bank's collapse. These put and call options gave the purchaser the right to sell and buy the index respectively at a set level (the strike price) over a given period of time. This strategy is known as a strangle or straddle, depending on the strike prices. This provided him with an inflow of cash, or premium, up front. No payment needed to be made to the buyer of the options until the end of their life, and then only if they held some intrinsic value which was determined by the level of the index at that time. The cost of this borrowing was the risk that the Nikkei 225 would move unfavourably against him. So long as the Nikkei 225 remained within a specific trading range, between the levels at which Leeson had sold the put and call options, he was in no danger of losing money and the premium he had collected would result in pure profit.

From the beginning of 1994, Leeson wrote so-called 'straddles', a bet that the index would trade only in a narrow range. The straddle is one of the most aggressive techniques for shorting volatility and exposes the option writer to considerable risk where markets move in a sudden and unexpected fashion. It appears, however, that Leeson made no attempt to hedge his portfolio, as the profit and loss swings correlate closely to moves in the index over this period.

Leeson gradually built up his positions over many months during a time of poor liquidity and relatively inactive market conditions. The Tokyo stock market trading volume from March to December of 1994 was close to an eight-year low and with the lack of any external stimulus, the index remained in a narrow trading range. These conditions were perfect for Leeson's strategy. The low volatility in the market reduced his chances of having to pay out when the options expired; so long as the market continued to trade between around 19,000 and 21,000 he was home and dry.

Leeson's prospects began to take a nose-dive in early 1995 when an anticipated New Year market rally failed to materialize as stocks came under selling pressure. The continued poor liquidity in the stock market exacerbated this weakness and the index gradually slid to the bottom of his trading range in mid-January. However, volatility remained low and looked likely to continue so. It was clear that it would take a significant change in investor sentiment or an external shock to lift the market out of its torpor.

The final analysis of the losses accrued when the bank was wound-up show that significant bets were taken beyond Leeson's Nikkei strategy. He was also trading in Japanese interest-rate and currency derivatives; staff and investigators who unravelled his positions found that Account 88888 had a short position of 26,079 Japanese Government bond futures contracts and 6,845 Euroyen contracts, but it was certainly his Nikkei trading strategies and most prominently his futures positions that were to cause the most extensive damage.

Leeson had not reckoned with the forces of nature. The trouble began in the early hours of 17 January when the great Hanshin earthquake rocked Japan's industrial heartland around Kobe and

Osaka, reaching a mammoth 7.2 on the Richter scale. The damage was immense. Over 5,000 lives were lost. In the immediate aftermath, the Nikkei dropped only slightly – the 225 futures contract fell from 19,350 on the day of the quake to 18,950 on Friday 20 January – as the prevailing sentiment was that the stimulus from reconstruction could probably offset the immediate disruption to production. Leeson must have watched with bated breath as the market hovered nervously around 19,000 that Friday.

As the bill for the damage scaled colossal heights, sentiment changed drastically over the weekend. On Monday, 23 January, the bottom got knocked out of the stock market when the Nikkei 225 dropped by over 1,000 points from 19,241 on the day of the quake to 17,785. Suddenly Leeson went berserk, but none of his trading counterparts were aware of the madness that had overcome him. His buying spree in Nikkei futures for Account 88888 following the Kobe earthquake was unprecedented by any standards. Within four weeks, his position on SIMEX had reached 55,399 contracts that expired in March and a further 5,640 in the June contract. These contracts left Barings with a loss in SIMEX of some Yen 59 billion (£384 million) as of Friday 25 February. There was also a long position in Osaka. The total loss on the options outstanding at 27 February 1995 was Yen 8.31 billion (£51 million).

Why did Leeson place such a huge bet? It is most likely that he was trying to shore up the market to restore the profitability of his straddles and other open positions. This assumes the apparently absurd premise that he could single-handedly hold up the Tokyo stock market during one of the greatest physical and financial disasters in Japanese history.

While Leeson was a hotshot in the trading pit in everyone's eyes, it is important to remember that he was relatively inexperienced, having only been trading on the floor for just over two years. Traders learn to adapt their trading style and to change tactics and strategies by experiencing different markets, volatile, one-way or quiet, for example. Leeson had never seen the phenomenon of the one-way market before. Steve Dagleish, a former trader who now works for the RDI consultancy group training traders to learn from their experiences, explains: 'You get used to a market which is always going to come back and suddenly you find yourself in a situation where it isn't going to, and you don't know how to cope with it. Over the last twenty or thirty years the Nikkei hasn't behaved itself. When it goes, it goes big time. If you're bucking the trend in most markets you get a chance, but in that one you obviously didn't. The question is how you feel when you think you've got an outside chance of it coming back and if it doesn't, how do you react then? An element of luck comes in, but where traders are counting on luck is where you've got problems.'

Leeson would certainly not be the first trader to panic in such a situation and follow the ridiculously unwise tradition of some hapless traders of doubling up to try to salvage an otherwise hopeless position. 'He basically had two options,' says one London derivatives trader. 'He could close out his positions to stop any further loss and tell Barings he'd dropped a bundle – in which case he could kiss his arse goodbye as far as his career was concerned. Or he could bet the bank and hope it came right. He probably reckoned he had nothing more to lose and went for broke.'

The uncovering of how Leeson successfully concealed his trades until the eleventh hour reveals a confusing web of deception that was ingenious in its complexity. In order to maintain the reported profitability of the authorized inter-exchange arbitrage business, Leeson made unauthorized adjustments to the price of transactions concluded on the SIMEX floor, allowing trades to be entered into the books and records of Baring Futures (Singapore) which were not genuine transactions. He did this by using 'cross trades', a transaction whereby a dealer buys and sells the same futures contracts, either on behalf of two of its clients, or between clients' accounts and the house account. This transaction should be concluded across the exchange floor. Baring Futures entered into a vast number of cross trades between Account 88888 and Accounts 92000, 98007, and 98008, the legitimate arbitrage accounts in Baring Securities (London) and Baring Securities (Japan).

After the conclusion of the trade, Leeson instructed the settlements staff to credit the profits to the authorized accounts and the losses to 88888. While on the exchange floor the cross trades appeared to be genuine, the books and records of Baring Futures showed pairs of transactions adding up to the same number of contract lots, but at prices which bore no absolutely no relation to those executed on the floor. In addition, he entered into fictitious trades between those accounts which were never crossed on the exchange floor, again crediting the legitimate switching accounts with profits while booking the losses to 88888.

Leeson also manipulated the Baring Futures books and records to deceive SIMEX about the true balance on 88888 by creating false journal entries, fabricating transactions and writing options. This fudging of the accounts and alteration or manufacturing of documents appears to have begun as early as September 1992 and successfully deceived external and internal auditors, as well as management.

However, his juggling with both house and client accounts, money and positions that had kept the internal controllers and external auditors at bay for so long, had begun to fall apart before the end of 1994. Leeson had failed to cover up a Yen 7.7 billion (£50 million) shortfall in the accounts that resulted from his unreported trading. Although he had been able to quickly find a solution to resolve this discrepancy within a few days by fudging the accounts to get the internal controllers off his back, the amount still needed justifying on the year-end accounts that were formally audited by Coopers & Lybrand in February 1995, but were never signed off due to outstanding unanswered questions.

The Singapore extradition documents sent to Germany allege that Leeson got around the problem by forging documents. Of the twelve charges of forgery and cheating, at least two relate to this covert Yen 7.7 billion. One of the papers is a letter purporting to show that Baring Futures had received Yen 7.8 billion from Spears, Leeds & Kellogg, the US investment firm, for the alleged execution of a call option on the Nikkei 225. The other document is a confirmation from Citibank in Singapore saying that Baring Futures received the money. Internal Barings' documents reportedly show that the accrued loss of Yen 7.7 billion built up by Leeson in 88888 by the end of 1994 was camouflaged as a receivable. Over the weekend of the crash, the Barings team forced open a drawer in Leeson's desk at Baring Futures. Tony Railton has described how 'there was a stack of papers. There were holes in some. You could see how he had produced [the] confirmation of the SLK deal, I believe, and also I think a bank statement as well.' Tony Gamby recalls 'we found some cut-and-paste material for the SLK transaction. There was this SLK letter with a scissor cut around the signature . . . we also found a cut-and-paste of the Citibank statement.' Papers found in Leeson's office also allegedly indicate that he had been practising the signature of Mr Richard Hogan, Managing Director of Spear Leeds & Kellogg.

In January 1995, Coopers & Lybrand informed Barings of this supposed transaction which was discussed internally. It created extreme confusion amongst management, but although the potential implications were that Leeson had involved himself in an unauthorized activity with obvious credit and risk implications, there was no detailed investigation to ascertain precisely what had happened.

By January 1995 Barings' index arbitrage positions and Leeson's huge trading volume on SIMEX had caused rumours to run rife in the market as to who Barings was acting for. It was assumed by everyone in the market that Barings must be in league with a big investor because nobody believed there was sufficient profitability to be made from index arbitrage to justify such a colossal build-up in positions. Nobody that is, except the management at Barings.

The scale of Leeson's trading activities entertained market participants and observers for weeks. They reached wildly varying conclusions about their origins. 'We thought they were doing it on behalf of American hedge funds,' says a source at the Japanese broking firm Nomura Securities. A US trader relates how: 'We always thought this was a Japanese client who was going to go bankrupt because his business was collapsing.'

Leeson himself nurtured these rumours. He created a myth that he was trading on behalf of clients who would speak to him directly on the floor of SIMEX. Legitimate names were chosen because they were 'give-up' clients, a classification that means Barings executed their trades while settlement was completed by another broker. He played on the fact that clients commonly request anonymity to help minimize the spread of rumours in the market regarding their investment activities. Some of these illegitimately used client names were chosen by Leeson because they had at one time been genuine, active clients of Barings, but were no longer, thus increasing the plausibility of his cover-up.

Early in 1994, Heather Nicol of the Financial Products Group in New York introduced Leeson to one such execution-only client, a trading entity named European Bank & Trust Limited, and he built up a relationship with Philippe Bonnefoy (known only as 'Philippe' to the Financial Products Group and management) an EBT trader. Leeson claimed to be executing large Nikkei 225 option orders for him up to the bank's crash, but EBT has since confirmed that it only traded through Leeson from the beginning of 1994 till June 1994.

Exchange traders in Singapore have also said that Leeson put it around that George Soros was backing him and that he therefore had a practically inexhaustible supply of money, another hoax that was merely designed to enhance his credibility.

However, while some were bemused by the scale of Leeson's dealings, there were many who were concerned. SIMEX alerted the company to the scale of its positions early in 1995, writing to Baring Futures on 27 January with a summary of its positions at 30 December 1994 and reminding it about its responsibility to ensure that it had sufficient funds to meet its obligations to the exchange. This letter was discussed at an ALCO meeting in London on the 31st, but the members felt there was no cause for concern.

The firm had been given a bigger warning signal on 11 January 1995, when SIMEX wrote to Simon Jones questioning the fact that Baring Futures appeared to be financing the positions of clients, in particular those in Account 88888. However, the matter was not communicated to London at that time, which therefore failed to follow it up. Moreover, although the reply was signed by Jones, it was, according to Jones, substantially drafted by Leeson.

In late January and February these market concerns and rumours escalated, precipitating a call on 27 January from the Bank for

International Settlements in Basle, which had heard rumours to the effect that the bank could not meet its margin calls. Even Barings' rivals contacted the bank. William Phillips, Managing Director of Salomon Brothers, Hong Kong and the former Head of Baring Securities Hong Kong had heard that if the Nikkei index reached 17,800 either Barings or a client of Barings would be bankrupt. He called the bank ten days before the crash to express his anxiety but was told that there was no outright exposure. At least one US bank cut off its dealings with Barings and another British broking firm put out a company-wide informal warning about dealing with the firm.

At Barings' London headquarters, however, all was relatively calm. The management were aware of the market rumours, but although the executives knew that the positions on the Japanese arbitrage book had ballooned after the earthquake, it did not cause them undue concern because they believed that the positions were fully hedged on SIMEX and thus risk-free. Indeed, they were more worried about how to tackle the publicity aspects rather than the positions themselves. They seem to have made no attempt, however, to investigate the rumours to the extent of checking that the positions were in fact matched.

Although there was no suspicion that directional bets had been taken on the Nikkei, ALCO members expressed concern about the size of the futures positions. The minutes of their meeting on 26 January 1995 record the instruction that 'Leeson to be advised that position should not be increased, and when possible reduced.' However, because Leeson was netting out the long Nikkei position against the short position in the Baring Securities (Japan) switching account, he could not afford to do this or SIMEX would have made a significant margin call. Consequently, despite the ALCO resolution, Leeson's positions ballooned in mid-February, but there appears to have been no investigation on the part of ALCO as to this breach of its strategy.

In the early part of 1995, as Leeson's unauthorized trading mushroomed, the funding required for margin at SIMEX, which was already high, increased dramatically. Leeson went to considerable lengths to reduce these margin calls, instructing his settlements staff from January to alter the positions in accounts 92000 and 88888 on the papers sent daily to SIMEX, thus deceiving the exchange as to the total amount of margin required on customer and house positions. Despite these moves, however, the funding continued to escalate; the cumulative funding of Baring Futures (Singapore) which stood at £221 million on 31 December 1994 had reached an epic £742 million by 24 February. This represented more than twice the reported capital of the Barings Group.

From the outside and with hindsight it seems staggering that such vast sums of money could have been sent out to fund Leeson's trading activities without anyone finding out that it was being used for hidden trades. Tony Hawes, Group Treasurer, has told the Bank of England: 'It was generally accepted that if possible we should put more funding in place. It was something that was accepted by the Asset & Liability Committee.' He added: 'We just accepted his [Leeson's] word that the figures required ran into millions. Yes, we just about accepted what he said.'

The millions of pounds sent out to Singapore were arranged by the group treasury in London and remitted by the futures and options settlements, while in Tokyo Baring Securities (Japan) approved the funding, which was remitted to Singapore by its own treasury. It was sent without any clear understanding on the part of management as to on whose behalf the monies were to be applied and without any real demur. No one understood whether, or to what extent, the sums requested by Baring Futures were for client trading or house trading, as there was no complete system to reconcile clients' debits with total positions. It assumed the balance went to house positions without checking whether the margin payments matched the positions.

The treasury and settlements departments were worried about their inability to reconcile the accounts and the fact that inadequate information for the funding requests was being provided by Baring Futures, particularly regarding the breakdown of Leeson's US dollar funding requests, the majority of which supported his unauthorized trades. Brenda Granger, Manager Futures and Options Settlements, recalled a conversation she had with Leeson about his dollar requests. She said to him, 'You're asking me for more money than I can collect in; so it is looking as if I have client debtors, which I do not.' To which he allegedly replied: 'Brenda, London is the cash cow. You are funding Singapore.' However, despite the anxieties of those in the settlements and treasury departments, the funds continued to be paid without any independent check on their validity or any concerted attempt to reconcile the requests to trading positions.

Spurred by concerns over the mounting funding requests, Tony Hawes and Tony Railton travelled to Singapore in the second week of February to question Leeson. There were several items on their list, including getting to the bottom of the Spears, Leeds & Kellogg cock-up, a response to SIMEX's need for reassurance about Barings' ability to fund its payments, and an in-depth investigation as to exactly where all the margin money was going. Hawes had visited Singapore in October to talk to Leeson about his futures trading activities, but at the last minute Leeson had made arrangements to be in London. In November, and again in January, Hawes had reiterated the importance of a trip to Singapore, but despite the commissioning of further reports and the fact that he had relayed his concerns to Ian Hopkins, Head of Group Treasury and Risk, no visit had taken place.

When Hawes finally arrived in Singapore, he easily reassured SIMEX officials that Barings could provide for its commitments. The matter of SLK did not seem urgent so he travelled on to Tokyo, intending to sort it out on his return. In the meantime, he left Leeson a list of questions.

During the following week Railton tackled the breakdown of the margin requirements and quickly realized there was a serious problem. He later recalled thinking, 'If you close out all the positions there is no way on God's earth that you could actually return all the yen.' His investigations revealed that his concerns about the breakdown of the US dollar margin funding requests submitted by Leeson to London were valid as Leeson's explanation was meaningless. He pestered Leeson for a meeting and was relieved when he finally agreed to see him on Monday 21 February, but on that

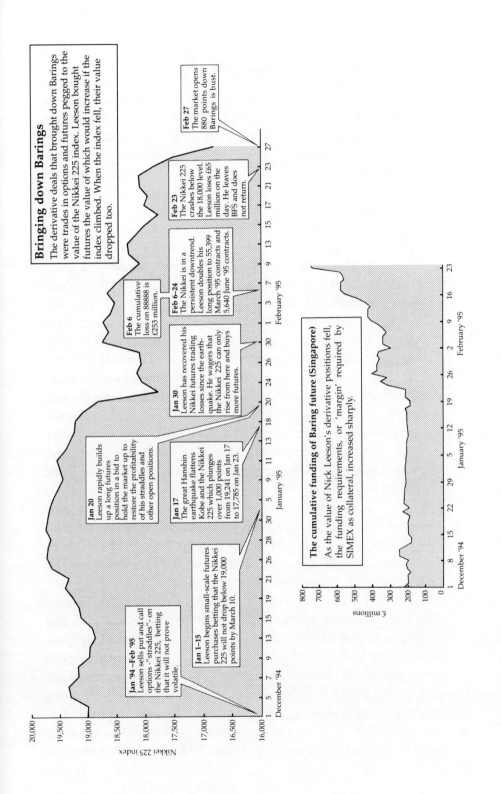

Bringing down Barings

The derivative deals that brought down Barings were trades in options and futures pegged to the value of the Nikkei 225 index. Leeson bought futures the value of which would increase if the index climbed. When the index fell, their value dropped too.

Nikkei 225 index

20,000
19,500
19,000
18,500
18,000
17,500
17,000
16,500
16,000

December '94   January '95   February '95

5 7 9 13 15 19 21 26 28 30 5 9 11 13 18 20 24 26 30 1 3 7 9 13 15 17 21 23 27

Jan '94–Feb '95
Leeson sells put and call options – "straddles" – on the Nikkei 225, betting that it will not prove volatile.

Jan 1–15
Leeson begins small-scale futures purchases betting that the Nikkei 225 will not drop below 19,000 points by March 10.

Jan 20
Leeson rapidly builds up a long futures position in a bid to hold the market up to restore the profitability of his straddles and other open positions.

Jan 17
The great Hanshin earthquake flattens Kobe and the Nikkei 225 which plunges over 1,000 points from 19,241 on Jan 17 to 17,785 on Jan 23.

Jan 30
Leeson has recovered his Nikkei futures trading losses since the earthquake. He wagers that the Nikkei 225 can only rise from here and buys more futures.

Feb 6
The cumulative loss on 88888 is £253 million.

Feb 6–24
The Nikkei is in a persistent downtrend. Leeson doubles his long position to 55,399 March '95 contracts and 5,640 June '95 contracts.

Feb 23
The Nikkei 225 crashes below the 18,000 level. Leeson loses £65 million on the day. He leaves BFS and does not return.

Feb 27
The market opens 880 points down Barings is bust.

The cumulative funding of Baring future (Singapore)

As the value of Nick Leeson's derivative positions fell, the funding requirements, or 'margin' required by SIMEX as collateral, increased sharply.

£ millions

800
700
600
500
400
300
200
100
0

December '94   January '95   February '95

1 8 15 22 29 5 12 19 26 2 9 16 23

Monday and Tuesday Leeson was reported ill and failed to appear.

Hawes and Railton's visit to Singapore had a side effect. Coopers & Lybrand, the accountancy firm which took over as auditor of Baring Futures (Singapore) in August 1994, had been about to sign off on the unit's accounts. After Hawes' visit, however, the auditors expressed concern that something in the picture did not seem quite right. They held off signing the accounts until they could clear up a few points with Leeson – but that meeting never took place.

By that stage Leeson was under mounting pressure. It was becoming increasingly difficult for him to conceal the scale of the losses and the flows of money required from London to cover margin calls. Yet he continued to act calmly, his sang-froid carrying into both his work and social life.

Critics have said that the arbitrage team in Tokyo should have been the first to smell a rat if there was one, but Leeson's remarkably consistent subterfuge maintained the illusion of normality not only to them but amongst all concerned. Leeson was his usual chatty self on the squawk box to the Tokyo traders from Barings booth down on SIMEX. Right up to Leeson's last morning on the trading floor he opened his conversation with Fernando Gueler, the Head Proprietary Equity Derivatives Trader in Tokyo, with his usual 'How's life?' Both his fellow floor traders on SIMEX and his trading counterparts in Tokyo say that he appeared completely normal. It was this constant charade that has left a confusion of fond memories with a bitter sting in his trading counterparts' minds. 'He was systematically lying for two years under the pretence of doing client trades. It leaves you with a bitter taste in your mouth thinking about it all now,' one of his fellow traders in Tokyo said to me.

Leeson maintained his composure in his social life too. It seems even Lisa was unaware of the problems Nick was facing as they planned a trip with three of his friends on the weekend of 25–26 February to celebrate his birthday, made other birthday party arrangements and invited a friend to stay with them in Singapore in a few weeks' time. Beneath this chirpy facade, the Leesons were privately making plans to leave Singapore. As far as Lisa was concerned, they were returning to England because Nick was burnt out; the plan was that once the bonus had been paid they would spend the summer recharging their batteries and deciding their future.

In accordance with this plan, Nick had sold his black Rover and was driving a white Mercedes, borrowed from a friend who had been temporarily seconded to Hong Kong. Lisa had contacted a removal company to arrange transport of their possessions back to England. On 15 February, ten days before the bank went under, Diane Massimiani of the Singapore removal firm Four Winds, was asked to arrange transport and storage of items from the couple's Singapore flat to West Kingsdown in Kent where Lisa's parents live. Barings' head office, meanwhile, had no idea of the Leeson's plans. On 20 February, Massimiani received another phone call saying that they might be going home earlier than expected. A third phone call on 24 February, from a woman who described herself as a friend of the couple, instructed Massimiani to have all their belongings packed and shipped to England on Wednesday, 1 March.

Unbeknownst to Lisa, this series of phone calls uncannily paralleled Barings' escalation of concern about Nick's trading activities: Tony Hawes was about to return from his side trip and would be looking to Nick to throw some light on the SLK affair; Coopers & Lybrand, perplexed at a mounting number of unanswered questions, had requested a meeting with Leeson; and Tony Railton was determined to get to the bottom of an unexplained shortfall in Nick's trading account.

Leeson's hoax was maintained to the end. Rushing off the floor on several occasions that morning, as he had done throughout that week, in order to vomit, Leeson told colleagues he had an upset stomach. The stress of concealment had been playing havoc with his health for some time. A friend from Hong Kong later remembered having a drink with him on a trip to Singapore last autumn, when he was surprised to see Nick order a shandy [half-lager, half-lemonade]. 'That's unusual for you isn't it?' he commented. 'I've just been to the hospital. I've got another ulcer,' Leeson replied. Colleagues in Singapore say that he had suffered from ulcer problems for some time.

That Thursday morning, after calling his friends from the

SIMEX floor to say that he could no longer make the weekend trip, Leeson gathered up his notes as usual at the end of the trading session and walked off the floor. That afternoon he sat down with Railton and Jones to discuss the matter of the missing money, but walked out in the middle of the meeting never to return.

Nick and Lisa left Singapore three years after they had arrived with so much promise. The next day, Friday 24 February, a handwritten letter from Leeson was faxed to Bax and Jones in Singapore from the Regent Hotel in Kuala Lumpur, where he had just checked in. It begins: 'My sincere apologies for the predicament that I have left you in. It was neither my intention or aim for this to happen but the pressures, both business and personal, have become too much to bear and after receiving medical advice, have affected my health to the extent that a breakdown is imminent.' The letter said he was tendering his resignation immediately, and promised to make contact early in the following week 'to discuss the best course of action', a promise that was never kept. The fax is signed 'Apologies, Nick.'

After Leeson's departure, the hall of mirrors which he had established to maintain his subterfuge came crashing down.

Blood Sport

Epilogue

Official inquiries into the circumstances of the collapse of Barings conducted by the Bank of England at the request of Kenneth Clarke, the Chancellor of the Exchequer, and by the Singaporean authorities began in the immediate aftermath of the bank's demise – a case, perhaps, of slamming the stable door after the horse has bolted. The reports were produced without any help from Nick Leeson, who was in a German prison pending resolution of an application for his extradition to Singapore. Leeson was invited to co-operate with the Bank's inquiry but declined to do so initially so long as he remained liable to be extradited to Singapore rather than the UK. He was informed of the Bank's conclusions as to his part in the collapse, to which his lawyer, Stephen Pollard of Kingsley Napley, replied: 'These conclusions are inaccurate in various respects. Indeed, in relation to certain matters they betray a fundamental misunderstanding of the actual events.'

Leeson later provided the Serious Fraud Office with a dossier of information incriminating himself, and offered himself up for interview by the SFO in a desperate attempt to be extradited from his Frankfurt prison cell to Britain. Pollard said, 'The inevitable conclusion of the high-risk strategy that Nick Leeson has adopted is that he would plead guilty in Britain to the charges he has supplied evidence on if he were brought back here.' The SFO at first rejected his request, despite reassurances that there were no strings attached, sticking to their line that he should be tried in the country where the alleged crimes were committed.

*   *   *

Nick Leeson's unauthorized trading activities were the catalyst for the collapse of Barings. He stands accused of fabricating and shredding documents relating to his trading activities, juggling accounts, money and positions, lying to auditors and management, falsifying trading reports to the Singapore exchange authorities, and dodging meetings with senior Barings executives seeking clarification of his activities. However, the final analysis of the events which led to the bank's failure reveals a catalogue of errors and omissions across the board. There were seven lines of defence which should have prevented it: management; external and internal auditors; regulatory bodies in Singapore, Tokyo and Osaka; and the Bank of England.

Barings was brought down by incompetence within the bank. Despite numerous warning signals about Leeson's ability to override internal controls and about his disastrous derivatives speculation in Singapore, and in spite of expressions of concern at high level in the bank and several visits to Singapore to clarify concerns, management failed to take action to staunch the huge loss-making trading in time to save the bank. The points of failing include the following:

- Management failed to segregate Leeson's duties; throughout he was permitted to remain in charge of both the front and back offices, despite warnings of the dangers inherent in this position in an internal audit. Management simply assumed that the recommendations attached would be acted upon. They were not.
- Senior executives and settlements staff failed to ensure that £742 million – over twice the bank's reported capital – sent out to fund Leeson's derivatives speculation, actually matched client accounts or the bank's own positions as declared by Leeson. They failed to pick up on this because there was no complete reconciliation of Barings' books. In spite of concerns, Barings settlement and treasury departments were never able to reconcile the 'top-up payments' demanded by Leeson, and made no effective attempt to clarify exactly where the money was being directed.

- Neither top management or the relevant members of the derivatives group understood the business that Leeson was supposed to be undertaking, despite vast reported profits and funding requirements. Leeson appeared to be making huge sums from what was deemed to be an essentially risk-free arbitrage business, but despite the fact that this goes against the well-established risk–reward ratio in investment banking there was no informed analysis or appraisal of this issue. As a result, they failed to introduce effective limits on either his trading or his funding requirements. According to the internal audit report of August 1994, there were 'no gross limits set for arbitrage positions . . . the only constraint is that group treasury will eventually inform Baring Futures that they will cease funding requirements if they grow too large.'

- Management failed to conduct a serious investigation of Leeson's activities despite market rumours throughout January and February 1995, and expressions of concern at high level from reputable sources, including the Bank for International Settlements. They also neglected to follow up adequately on a letter from SIMEX to Baring Futures pointing out irregularities in Account 88888 or to look into a discrepancy in the Singapore accounts – a receivable of £50 million – for which external auditors noted that there was insufficient documentation.

Although many key management decisions were taken on the basis of inaccurate information provided by Leeson and within an environment with inadequate controls, management has admitted its culpability on this front. Ron Baker told the Bank of England investigators: 'There is no doubt in my mind, that my lack of experience in the area was a contributing factor to what has happened here [the collapse]. All I can say in defence of that is that lack of experience is something that I have overcome before in my life when I have taken things on, but if you ally lack of experience to the lack of information I got and to the other failures in the organization, in the failure to give me accurate information . . . then I think that meant getting up a learning curve which was impossible. There is no doubt in my mind that if I had had ten years' experience in exchange-traded equity derivatives, this would not have happened. The fact is, I did not.' He added that his lack of experience did not mean he was the wrong person for the job, but it made him more reliant on the control and information systems than he would otherwise have been.

Although there can be no excuse for management's short-comings, it is important to recognize that Leeson's unauthorized activities took place against the backdrop of an ambitious internal reconstruction involving the integration of the bank and the brok-ing operations. During this state of flux, the organization was in a position of considerable vulnerability; adequate controls were not put in place quickly enough for management to detect the trading losses. George Maclean, head of Bank Group, has commented: 'I believe the seeds of this [the collapse] were sown when we went into Baring Securities Ltd to bring the two companies together and made the assumption that the quality controls that we [Baring Brothers] had could quickly get installed there. As it turned out, that appears not to be true.'

The process of integration engendered ambiguity within the new organization; lines of reporting and responsibility were not clearly defined, resulting in confusion and a pervasive lack of management control. During the restructuring a large number of employees were put in positions of theoretical responsibility, but in many cases did not understand that responsibility or were not empowered to fulfil the roles given to them. Management structures became tangled and Leeson fell through one of the gaps.

One example of such confusion about responsibility was the Board of Directors of Baring Futures (Singapore). The Board was composed of six members: James Bax, Fu Ya-Yin, Roy Johnson, Simon Jones, Peter Norris and Mike Killian. Few of these directors took an active part in the running of the company; in fact, some were not even familiar with the details of the business conducted. There have been suggestions that their lack of involvement should imply less direct responsibility, but the Singapore authorities were resolute in their response to this proposal. The local regulators' attitude is that if those in positions of responsibility are unable or unwilling to fulfil their roles they should step down in favour of a more able candidate.

Aad Jacobs, ING's Chairman, and Hessel Lindenberg, the man who was given the task of handling ING's takeover of the crashed Barings empire, made it clear that it was the new owners' preference to wait until the Bank of England's inquiry report was available before judging individuals' responsibility for the collapse and taking management action. 'We did not agree to pay almost £700 million to acquire a people business if we did not expect to keep the people on board,' said Aad Jacobs. 'We are not going to fire anyone.'

However, publication of Part One of the Bank of England's report – an analysis of what went wrong at Barings – originally scheduled for six to eight weeks after the bank's collapse, was postponed first to June and then to July, causing outrage both in and outside the bank. Although the preliminary report was ready in June, the Treasury at that point maintained that there were never plans to publish it separately from Part Two which included lessons to be learnt from the affair. That delay caused uncertainty both internally amongst staff and externally among clients, and even the general public, as to which executives would remain, an uncertainty that began to hinder ING's attempts to relaunch Barings. ING was therefore forced to take a hard, but pragmatic, move in seeking the resignations of those considered responsible for controlling the activities of Leeson whose actions were deemed to have caused Barings' demise. Although there has never been any suggestion that those who left had committed criminal offences, they were nevertheless forced to pay the price of the bank's collapse with their jobs and possibly careers. Further to an inquiry by the Securities and Futures Authority, the Barings executives criticized in the Bank of England report face possible removal from the SFA's register, preventing them from re-employment by other securities businesses in the UK.

On 3 April 1995, Peter Baring and Andrew Tuckey fell on their swords when ING accepted their resignations as the Chairman and Deputy Chairman respectively of Barings plc. At the request of ING and his colleagues, Tuckey agreed to remain as a senior advisor to Barings' corporate finance business with which he had been particularly associated.

Due to the absurd length of delay in the Bank of England's report, and the possibility that, for fear of being made to look foolish by the results of the seemingly more thorough investigation carried out by the Singapore authorities, the Bank would wait even longer, ING was forced to take further steps towards reassuring staff and clients. On 1 May 1995 ING accepted the resignations of twenty-one more individuals: eleven in London, three in Singapore and seven in Tokyo, who according to Lindenberg 'comprised the executives of the firm with functional responsibility (whether direct or indirect) for the Singapore derivatives business.'

The departed individuals included four closely associated with Leeson: Peter Norris, Ron Baker, Simon Jones and James Bax. Norris had already stepped down as chief executive officer of Baring Securities Ltd but had remained as an advisor. Lindenberg said ING decided to clean the slate then to shore up the confidence of both staff and clients in the new operation. 'Our review has confirmed that the problem stemming from Singapore was extraordinary and not endemic. It is a problem we have put behind us. We now turn our attention to the future,' said Lindenberg. 'Our goal is fully to restore the pre-eminence of the Barings name and to build the businesses, which are now again well capitalized, through providing our clients with first class service from a first class organization.' Lindenberg accompanied the announcement with the statement that: 'It is with no pleasure that we have said goodbye to those who have left. Those who have departed have given many years of loyal service to Barings.'

While management must bear the brunt of criticism for allowing Leeson's activities to continue unchecked, external regulators also deserve censure. The complete absence of communication between the exchanges in Japan and Singapore, and the poor contact between the exchanges and Barings undoubtedly played its part in the bank's collapse. At no time did SIMEX independently contact the Osaka Exchange to verify Barings' explanation that its

Singapore exposure was hedged with positions on the Japanese exchange, a simple procedure which might have saved the bank. Despite the rivalry of these exchanges, it seems extraordinary that, according to Osaka officials, they have only met their SIMEX counterparts three times in seven years, a level of communication which is remarkable given that the two exchanges share similar contracts. However, communication between exchanges around the world has traditionally been poor, so Osaka and SIMEX were not exceptional in this respect. Since the collapse, a number of initiatives have been taken by regulatory bodies to improve international co-operation and information sharing.

Communication between the exchanges and Barings was equally bad. The Osaka Exchange made no attempt to approach Barings at any time, despite the scale of the positions it was building up through January and February, and has said that it would not do so in the future. SIMEX made considerably more effort to contact Barings during January and February, providing Simon Jones with full details of Baring Futures' open positions at SIMEX, as of 30 December 1994, on 27 January, and pointing out to the firm irregularities in Account 88888 in a letter to Baring Futures on 11 January. It accepted oral and written statements from Barings, and failed to probe in depth the futures positions Leeson was accumulating, in spite of growing alarm on the part of Exchange officials at the size of the positions. The Exchange simply relied on the bank's good name and credit standing. Since the crash, Elizabeth Sam, the Chairwoman of SIMEX has said, 'We have learned not to accept explanations at face value, notwithstanding the firm. If this incident has highlighted anything, it is the importance of exchanges being able to communicate with one another.'

The Bank of England has got off too lightly in its own analysis of the collapse. While the Board of Banking Supervision's report was liberal in its blame, spreading it lavishly around Barings management and its auditors as well as Leeson, the bank itself came off relatively unscathed. Although it made seventeen recommendations for tightening aspects of its supervision, it stated that no fundamental change in the framework of financial regulation in the UK was required.

One of the central concerns is how the Bank monitored the capital adequacy and large exposures of Barings' banking and securities businesses. The Bank did not fully assess the impact of, or address all the issues related to supervising the Barings Group on a so-called solo consolidation basis in which one set of capital and exposure standards are applied to both the parent bank and its securities subsidiaries. In Barings' case, the linkage was the first time a substantial securities company had been solo consolidated with the bank in the UK.

The second most glaring failure was the way Barings was allowed to overstep its capital restrictions. A key aspect of the Bank's supervision for purposes of monitoring credit risk are the large exposure rules it sets which include a requirement that the Bank of England should be notified in the event that a bank's proposed exposures will exceed 25 per cent of its own or its group's capital base. In 1993 an informal concession was granted by a Bank of England official, permitting Barings to exceed this 25 per cent limit with regard to the Group's exposure to the OSE. It was also taken by Barings, unsurprisingly, to apply to its exposure to SIMEX. The granting of the concession, which was apparently made without reference to more senior management at the Bank, was criticized in the report as an error of judgment. No limit was at any time imposed on the concession. The Bank considered the issue for more than a year before revoking the concession in January 1995 and this delay may well have been a factor in Barings' collapse only weeks later.

The Bank of England had a number of means at its disposal for identifying problems at Barings, such as the annual report by Barings' auditors, Coopers & Lybrand, on the firm's management systems and controls, which includes such information as how the bank limits activities such as fraud. While such a report would cover high-level management and controls, however, it would not have covered the controls of Baring Futures directly. Such information should have been passed to them by the internal auditors. Apparently it was not.

Even if the Bank had not been told formally that borrowing to fund Leeson's positions was increasing rapidly, it might have picked up signals from the London money markets. At least one UK bank noticed that Barings was drawing on credit facilities from the end of January. Moreover, while rumours circulating in financial markets about Barings' positions had reached even the Bank for International Settlements, the Bank of England remained ignorant of Barings' difficulties until it was informed by Peter Baring. Its failure to pick up on these rumours in spite of its role in the money markets raises a serious question about its ability to detect problems.

The Bank's conclusion that no fundamental change in the framework for financial regulation was required caused outrage in the House of Commons: Gordon Brown, the Shadow Chancellor, called the report a 'damning indictment' of how the Bank views its supervisory role and demanded a review of its supervisory function. 'After three embarrassing failures – Johnson Matthey, BCCI and now Barings – we must do far more . . . to ensure that there is far greater confidence in the integrity of our financial system,' he said. While the Bank believes that it should retain its supervisory role, its oversights and lack of vigour in the Barings saga undermine its argument. There is now a strong case to be made for the Bank to retain only its monetary role, handing over supervision to an independent body as does the German Bundesbank.

Those in senior management at Barings who controlled (or failed to control) Leeson's trading activities and created the environment in which he operated, bear ultimate responsibility for allowing the bank to collapse. But this only explains why such a disaster was allowed to happen, not why it was Nick Leeson who made it happen.

Why did Nick Leeson make it happen? Without any valid explanation from him, it is impossible to ascertain the strategy (if there was one) or the motivation for his unauthorized trading. The possibility that other Barings employees or an outside party were involved with these activities still cannot be excluded, nor can the possibility that any of the funds forwarded by parts of the Barings Group to support those activities has been misappropriated.

Leeson himself has claimed altruistic motives: 'I did not steal any money. I hope that is clear to everybody. Everything I did was done in the hope that it would be for the ultimate benefit of the bank,' he told the world's media in a letter read out by his wife at a press conference on 12 July 1995 – an impassioned plea for him to be spared a 'show trial' in Singapore. 'I acted unwisely and exceeded my authority, but never with the intention of improperly enriching myself.' He claimed his 'biggest crime' was trying to protect colleagues, 'and ensure that the bonuses that they expected were paid and it is this that led to the escalation of the problem and the offences of which I now stand accused.'

It is unsurprising that Leeson would have us believe that this is the case, hoping to win the sympathy of the British public, traditional backers of the underdog, by convincing them that fate alone placed him in the hands of an inept management who tempted him to gamble with hundreds of millions of pounds. But against the backdrop of his systematic concealment of staggering trading losses dating back as far as 1992, his lawyer's suggestion that he would plead guilty, if brought back to London, to at least four charges of false accounting – crimes which would carry a sentence of up to fourteen years in Changi jail – and considered in light of the fact that he was prepared to walk away with a bonus of nigh on half a million pounds in full knowledge of the fact that it would have been obtained deceitfully, this is difficult to stomach. Leeson is not someone to feel sorry for. As a direct result of his unauthorized trading activities, the jobs of four thousand hard-working Barings employees were put in jeopardy, not to mention the life-savings lost by the private investors who bought Barings 'Perpetual Bonds'. There *are* genuine victims of Barings' collapse and Leeson is not one of them.

While he is not a victim to feel sorry for, neither is he an archvillain. Leeson may have been driven by his ego, a desire to be a big-shot in the eyes of his fellow traders and senior managers, he may have been motivated by the prospect of large bonuses for himself and his bosses or even by the avaristic desire to cream off a little extra for himself. But in any or all of the above scenarios, his behaviour was undoubtedly exacerbated by the macho trading environment in which he worked; an environment which is dominated by the financial and psychological rewards of success in the trading pit. While driven by the benefits of success however he quite clearly also succumbed to the flip side of this golden coin, the more destructive and dysfunctional forms of behaviour which result from fear of failure and humiliation.

Karen Weaving, a director of RDI, a consultancy specializing in organization development, corroborates this view: 'Nick probably found it difficult to admit earlier in the trading cycle that he was going to make a loss, so he hid from it. It was only when it slapped him in the face that he had to confront the enormity of his position. In any risk management situation like this the trader should have cut his losses a long time ago. So the question is: why didn't Nick? He was probably experiencing common distortions in his thinking patterns that are associated with high levels of stress: denying that the losses would ever occur and rejecting any type of information that indicated his position might be wrong. Many traders have admitted to me that they have experienced this type of defensive thinking and have made huge losses because of it.'

Leeson was not alone in his fear and denial. Such behavioural patterns are experienced by many in the City, including high-level management. 'A lot of senior executives, unless they've come up through the dealing route, will have, to a certain extent, lost familiarity with that type of culture and product, especially if you're talking about complex risk management,' says Karen Weaving. 'Again, rather than saying "we don't understand what's going on", chief executives often refuse to admit their lack of knowledge. This is quite common in a City banking culture. It takes leadership and courage to say as a Chief Executive "I do not understand what's going on in these markets; I do not understand derivatives." I think that many senior executives won't admit to their colleagues or to themselves that they are not in control of the situation either. This can lead to a whole cycle of events where everyone is not quite in control of the situation but they're all too scared to admit it.'

*   *   *

Leeson's activities and the bank's collapse should not be taken in isolation. To see the full picture you have to put his transgressions into the broader context of the financial industry as a whole. Leeson's trading losses reached the epic figure of £827 million, but the scenario is by no means unique. There are many other traders – far more than the general public would care to imagine – who have lost substantial amounts of their firm's money in bouts of bad, and sometimes unauthorized, trading. The public has not heard of *them* because the banks for which they were working had enough capital to swallow the losses and avoid damaging publicity. Barings simply did not have deep enough pockets to avoid its fate.

It was perhaps with this knowledge and fear in mind that in the immediate aftermath of the crash regulators and financial institutions alike scrambled to tighten controls and draw up lessons to be learnt from Barings' collapse in a bid to prevent a similar occurrence. But lessons were supposed to have been learnt in the past. In the wake of Barings' near-bankruptcy in 1890, Bertram Currie, a former friend of the Baring family who found himself conducting the Bank of England's investigation into the affair, wrote:

> If such colossal houses as those of Overend and Baring, the two greatest probably that I had known, paid the penalty of their imprudence, what man of business can with impunity depart from the beaten track? In both cases the evil probably began from a plethora of money attracted by the high credit which each house enjoyed. In the case of Messrs Baring, it was aggravated by a taste for extravagant expenditure and by the marvellous success which had attended some of their ventures.

Currie concluded that, 'for once my principles [in urging Barings' soundness] were at fault ... although in common with most discerning people I deplored the departure from sound traditions which was manifest to all observers ... I could not bring myself to believe that the resources and credit of the house of Baring were not equal to any strain. Let this example be a warning to my successors.'

Glossary

The scale of Nick Leeson's gambles was beyond the grasp of many people and so too was the jargon of the markets where he lost millions. This guide may help.

AGENCY BUSINESS See *client account* below.

ALCO Asset and Liability Committee (Barings plc).

ARBITRAGE Profiting from perceived temporary price differentials when the same security, currency or commodity is traded on two or more markets. INDEX ARBITRAGE exploits price differences between stock index futures and underlying stocks. At Barings the simultaneous purchase and sale of the same futures contracts on the different futures exchanges was known as 'switching'.

BACK OFFICE The department of a financial institution not directly involved in selling or trading. The back office is responsible for the processing and settling of trades and other administrative work.

CLEARING HOUSE An institution which registers, monitors, matches and guarantees trades on an exchange, and which settles the financial parts of these transactions.

CLEARING MEMBER A company which is a member of the futures clearing house. A clearing member must also be a member of the relevant exchange. Such firms can provide registration and settlement services for other exchange members who are not clearing members themselves.

CLIENT ACCOUNT An account held by a clearing member on behalf of its clients for their trading in securities or derivatives. Strict separation of client account balances from the *house account* (see below) is usually required by regulatory bodies. At Barings client business was known as agency business.

CME Chicago Mercantile Exchange (US).

CROSS TRADE A transaction whereby the same dealer buys and sells the same securities or futures contracts on behalf of two of its clients, or between *client accounts* and the *house account*. Most exchanges stipulate that this cross must be first offered to the market; it should therefore be concluded across the exchange floor for price visibility.

DERIVATIVES Financial instruments whose price is based on the expected movement in value of an underlying asset. Such assets can range from currencies, individual shares and stock market indices to commodities such as frozen orange juice. Derivatives usually cost a fraction of the underlying asset, making them highly geared. Thus, a small change in the underlying asset creates a volatile change in the derivative.

EUROYEN A yen-denominated financial instrument traded outside the formal control of the Japanese monetary authorities.

EXERCISE PRICE See *strike price*.

FRONT OFFICE The department of a financial institution where business is initiated, incorporating sales and trading.

FUTURES CONTRACT An agreement to buy or sell a specific amount of a commodity or financial instrument at a particular price on a stipulated date. The price is established between buyer and seller on the floor of an exchange or on a dealing room screen.

HEDGERS Users of derivatives whose main aim is to reduce their risk exposure.

HEDGING The use of derivatives to protect an open position in an underlying asset. It is not fail-safe and it now makes up just a small proportion of total global derivatives trading.

HOUSE ACCOUNT An account held by a financial institution to record trades made on the dealer's own account for profit or loss. A house account is used to segregate transactions made on behalf of clients from those made for the firm. See proprietary trading.

JGB Japanese Government Bond.

MARGIN The good-faith deposit that a client must lodge with a broker, or indeed that a broker must lodge with the exchange, when buying or selling a contract in order to cover any potential losses on his position. As the underlying asset moves, then the broker or exchange can demand that the client puts up more money (maintenance margin) to meet margin requirements.

MARGIN CALL A demand from an exchange, or from a broker carrying a client's position, for the financial institution/client to deposit additional money or collateral in respect of a position to bring a margin account up to the initial margin or minimum maintenance requirements. If an institution/client fails to respond, securities in the account may be liquidated.

MARK-TO-MARKET Adjusting the value of a security or portfolio to reflect current market values.

MATCHED POSITIONS Equal and offsetting long and short positions (see below).

NIKKEI 225 (Nikkei Stock Average/Nikkei Dow) An index based on the 225 leading Japanese stocks traded on the Tokyo Stock Exchange. It is composed of representative blue-chip companies and is a price-weighted index. This is the most popularly quoted stock index in Japan and the basis for the major Japanese equity derivative contracts.

OPEN OUTCRY A trading method whereby trading takes place in a designated area of the exchange known as a pit, within an agreed time-frame. The term derives from the fact that traders must shout out their buy or sell offers. When a trader shouts that he wants to sell at a particular price and someone else shouts that he wants to buy at that price, the two traders have made a contract that will be recorded by completing a ticket afterwards.

OPTION The right to buy or sell a commodity, currency or security on a set date that is granted in exchange for an agreed upon sum. If the right is not exercised after a certain period, the option expires and the option buyer forfeits the money. Options on financial futures take two forms: a PUT OPTION is a contract that grants the buyer the right, but not the obligation, to sell to the writer of the contract by a certain date a specified number of securities or derivatives at a specified price (the strike price). The put option buyer gains this right in exchange for an option premium. The put option seller grants this right in return for receiving this premium. Put buyers expect the price of the underlying security to fall. A CALL OPTION is a similar contract that grants the buyer the right, but not the obligation, to buy shares of a particular security or derivative from the option writer at a predetermined price before a preset deadline in return for a premium. A call buyer speculates that the price of the underlying instrument will rise.

OPTION PREMIUM The amount paid by an option buyer to an option seller for the right to buy (call) or sell (put) the underlying security at a particular price within a specified period.

OSE Osaka Securities Exchange (Japan).

OVER-THE-COUNTER (OTC) A security or financial instrument that is not listed and traded on an organized exchange. Transactions in such instruments are instead conducted through a telephone and computer network connecting dealers. Such instruments can be created within provisions allowed by law and which are acceptable to counter-parties.

P&L Profit and Loss

POSITION An investor's stake in a particular security or market. A long position equals the number of financial instruments owned; a short position equals the number of financial instruments owed.

PROPRIETARY TRADING The term used to describe risk positions taken by a firm for its own house account (see above) as distinct from those taken for clients.

SETTLEMENT The process by which a trade is entered into the books and records of all parties involved in the transaction. This includes completion of any payment between any of those parties related to the transaction.

SFA Securities and Futures Authority (UK).

SIMEX Singapore International Monetary Exchange.

SPAN MARGINING Standard Portfolio Analysis of risk: a system of determining margin (see above) used by SIMEX and some other exchanges.

SPECULATION The assumption of risk in anticipation of gain, while recognizing a higher than average possibility of loss.

STRADDLE A position created by combining an equal number of put options and call options (see above) on the same underlying stock, stock index or commodity future at the same strike price (see below) and maturity date. A seller of straddles anticipates that the underlying price will stay close to the level of the strike price of the options he has sold, or that the volatility of the price will be less than that implied in the option prices.

STRIKE PRICE The price at which the stock or commodity underlying a call or put option can be purchased (call) or sold (put) over the specified period. The strike price is usually set at the time the option contract is written.

SWITCHING See arbitrage above.

TSE Tokyo Stock Exchange (Japan).

WARRANT A form of option. It gives the owner the right to buy shares in a company at a fixed price and a fixed date in the future. If you own such a warrant and the share price rises above the exercise (strike) price, you are in profit. If it does not rise that high, the warrant is valueless, but there is no obligation to buy the underlying shares.

Index